About the series:

The books in the Routledge-Cavendish Essential series are intended as a helpful revision aid for both the undergraduate law student and non-law students studying law modules as part of their course. Written in a clear and accessible style, these books provide comprehensive yet succinct introductions to all of the major law subjects.

About the series editor:

Professor David Barker AM is based in the faculty of law at the University of Technology, Sydney.

Titles in the series:

Essential Administrative Law 3/e
Essential Australian Law 2/e
Essential Constitutional Law 2/e
Essential Corporate Law 2/e
Essential Criminal Law 3/e
Essential Dispute Resolution 2/e
Essential Evidence 3/e
Essential Family Law 3/e
Essential International Trade Law 2/e
Essential Jurisprudence
Essential Real Property
Essential Tort Law 3/e

Forthcoming titles in the series:

Essential Contract Law 3/e
Essential Equity & Trusts 2/e
Essential Professional Conduct: Legal Ethics 2/e

Essential Professional Conduct

Legal Accounting

Second Edition

BRONWYN OLLIFFE

Routledge
Taylor & Francis Group
LONDON AND NEW YORK

First published 2001 by Cavendish Publishing

Published 2018 by Routledge
2 Park Square, Milton Park, Abingdon, Oxon OX14 4RN
711 Third Avenue, New York, NY 10017, USA

First issued in hardback 2018

Routledge is an imprint of the Taylor & Francis Group, an informa business

Typeset in Helvetica by
Newgen Imaging Systems (P) Ltd, Chennai, India

British Library Cataloguing in Publication Data
A catalogue record for this book is available from the British Library

Library of Congress Cataloging in Publication Data
A catalog record for this book has been requested

ISBN 13: 978-1-138-37202-3 (hbk)
ISBN 13: 978-1-876905-34-7 (pbk)

Contents

Introduction

A knowledge of basic book-keeping is essential for every legal practitioner. In New South Wales, a law practice that has received trust money is required by the Legal Profession Act to account for clients' money. The Act imposes the conditions to account and the Legal Profession Regulation prescribes in great detail how this must be done.

The Legal Pofession Act 2004 was proclaimed to commence on 1 October 2005. This was also the date for the commencement of the Legal Profession Regulation 2005. This second edition has been updated in the light of the changes brought about by the recent legislation.

A solicitor in practice is also carrying on a business and must therefore meet the obligations of every person who carries on a business.

This book is an account of book-keeping procedures which will meet the requirements of the legislation. It is primarily intended to assist students studying degree or diploma courses in law and practical legal training. Other Professional Conduct topics are covered in the companion Cavendish text Essential Professional Conduct: Legal Ethics by Geoff Monahan. It is designed to assist those using manual book-keeping systems on the premise that those using computer systems must first understand the basic manual system. This book does not seek to explain accounting theory.

It is important that the newcomer to legal book-keeping begins the 'doing' as early as possible. With this in mind, a series of 'practice transactions' together with 'specimen accounts' have been provided. Once you have created the accounts of Potter and Associates, I am sure that any qualm you may have had about legal book-keeping will have been dismissed.

Bronwyn Olliffe
University of Technology, Sydney
December 2005

References

The Law Society of New South Wales, Legal Accounting Handbook Trust and Controlled Money, 5th edn, 2005, Sydney: Law Society of New South Wales.

Legislation
Legal Profession Act 2004 (NSW)
Legal Profession Regulation 2005 (NSW)

Abbreviations

ADI	Authorised deposit-taking institution within the meaning of the Banking Act 1959 of the Commonwealth
BSB	Bank State Branch number (each branch has a BSB number to distinguish branches of an ADI)
GST	Goods and Services Tax
LPA	Legal Profession Act
LPR	Legal Profession Regulation
NSW	New South Wales

1 Trust Money

Duty to account

When a solicitor receives money to be held on trust, the general law obligations of a trustee apply. The duties of a trustee which apply to a solicitor in relation to trust funds include:

- a duty to keep and render proper accounts and to give full information when required;
- a duty not to deal with the trust property for his/her own benefit, or otherwise to profit by the trust;
- a duty not to mix trust funds with his/her own funds or with other funds;
- a duty not to delegate his/her duties or powers.

In addition to these duties, in New South Wales a solicitor's obligations are regulated by statute. The Legal Profession Act 2004 (LPA) imposes the conditions to account for client's money and the Legal Profession Regulation 2005 (LPR) prescribes in detail how this should be done. While the Legal Profession Act 2004 and the Legal Profession Regulation 2005 are New South Wales legislations they are based on a national core model. It is intended that a practitioner will find similar provisions on trust money and trust accounts in every other state's equivalent legislation.

In relation to the trust account, the prime part of the LPA is in Chapter 3, Part 3. Part 3 begins with s 242 and here we find the purposes of this Part.

Section 242 purposes:

(a) to ensure trust money is held by law practices in a way that protects the interests of persons for or on whose behalf money is held, both inside and outside this jurisdiction;

(b) to minimise compliance requirements for law practices that provide legal services within and outside this jurisdiction;

(c) to ensure the Law Society Council can work effectively with corresponding authorities in other jurisdictions in relation to the regulation of trust money and trust accounts.

Definition of trust money

Trust money is defined in s 243 LPA. According to s 243, trust money means money received in the course of or in connection with the provision of legal services by a law practice for or on behalf of another person and includes:

(a) money received on account of legal costs in advance of providing the services; and

(b) controlled money; and

(c) transit money; and

(d) money controlled by a law practice (or by an associate, alone or with another associate) pursuant to a power to deal with money for or on behalf of another person that is

(i) exercisable by the practice (or by an associate alone or with another associate); or

(ii) exercisable jointly and severally with the person or a nominee or nominees of the person;

but does not include money to which s 244 applies.

This definition of trust money is not an exhaustive definition. The section specifically 'includes' four types of money that are trust money but does not limit itself to those categories. The money which is specifically excluded is money involved in financial services or investments as defined in s 244.

Categories of trust money

When a law practice has received trust money a decision must be made as to which type of trust money it is. The category of trust money will determine what is to be done with the money.

Under s 254 certain trust money is to be deposited in a general trust account.

According to s 254 (1), subject to s 258A as soon as practicable after receiving trust money, a law practice must deposit the money in a general trust account unless:

(a) the practice has a written direction by an appropriate person to deal with it otherwise than by depositing it in the account; or

(b) the money is controlled money; or

(c) the money is transit money; or

(d) the money is to be dealt with under a power to receive or disburse money for or on behalf of another person exercisable jointly or severally with the other person or a nominee of the other person.

Subject to s 258A, in those instances where the law practice receives money that is the subject of a written direction, it must deal with the money in accordance with that direction, within the period specified or if no period is specified, as soon as practicable after it is received. The law practice must keep a written direction mentioned in subsection (1)(a) for the period prescribed by the regulations.

Section 255 provides that a law practice must hold trust money deposited in a general trust account of the practice exclusively for the person on whose behalf it is received, disburse the trust money only in accordance with a direction given by the person, and account for the trust money as required by the regulations.

The keeping of trust records is dictated by s 264 LPA. A law practice must keep in permanent form trust records in relation to trust money received by the practice. Those records must be kept

(a) in accordance with the regulations; and
(b) in a way that at all times discloses the true position in relation to trust money received for or on behalf of any person; and
(c) in a way that enables the trust records to be conveniently and properly investigated or externally examined; and
(d) for a period determined in accordance with the regulations.

The aim of this section is to ensure that the law practice's accounting records at all times reflect the true position of each client's money.

General trust account

Section 253 LPA requires a law practice that receives trust money to which Part 3 of the LPA applies to maintain a general trust account in this jurisdiction in accordance with the regulations.

General trust account money covers money entrusted to the law practice in the course of or connection with the provision of legal services including money received on account of legal costs in advance of providing the services. It is money which according to s 254(1) must be deposited in a general trust account as soon as practicable after receiving it.

Written direction money

This type of trust money was a new category of trust money introduced to NSW practitioners by the Legal Profession Act 2004. It is referred to in s 254(1)(a). Under s 254(1)(a) a law practice is not required to pay this type of trust money into a general trust account. An exception to this is where the trust money is received in the form of cash. In s 258A we find:

1 Trust money (other than controlled money and money that is the subject of a power) received in the form of cash must be deposited in a general trust account of the law practice concerned.
2 If the law practice has a written direction by an appropriate person to deal with trust money referred to in subsection (1) otherwise than by depositing it in a general trust account of the practice, the trust money must be deposited in the general trust account before it is otherwise dealt with in accordance with the direction, despite anything to the contrary in the direction.

It is important to know who is an appropriate person to make a written direction. Section 254 (5) defines an appropriate person for the purpose of the section as a person legally entitled to give the law practice directions in respect of dealings with the trust money. This might include a person who is not a client of the law practice.

The written direction must be kept in the trust records of the law practice for seven years after the finalisation of the matter to which it relates.

Controlled money

The third category of trust money is controlled money. Section 256 LPA deals specifically with controlled money and provides:

1 As soon as practicable after receiving controlled money, a law practice must deposit the money in the account specified in the written direction relating to the money.

2 The law practice must hold controlled money deposited in a controlled money account in accordance with subsection (1) exclusively for the person on whose behalf it was received.

If the controlled money is received in the form of cash there is no requirement to pay it into the general trust account before complying with the written direction (see s 258A (3)).

The Legal Profession Act 2004 has changed the way in which the receipt of controlled money is managed by a law practice. The first difference is that now a written direction for the controlled money must be obtained. Section 256 further provides that the law practice must maintain the controlled money account, and account for the controlled money, as required by the regulations. We will further examine controlled money in Chapter 8.

Transit money

Where a law practice receives money which is subject to instructions to pay or deliver it to a third party, this money is described as transit money.

Transit money is the fourth category of trust money referred to in s 254(1)(c).The section of the Act which deals with transit money is s 257:

1 Subject to s 258A a law practice that has received transit money must pay or deliver the money as required by the instructions relating to the money;

(a) within the period (if any) specified in the instructions; or

(b) subject to paragraph (a), as soon as practicable after it is received.

2 The law practice must account for the money as required by the regulations.

If transit money is received in the form of cash then it must first be paid into the general trust account (s 258A).

Clause 81 of the LPR provides in subsection 2 that a law practice must, in respect of transit money, record and retain brief particulars sufficient to identify the relevant transaction and any purpose for which money was received.

Although a transit money register is not specified, law practices keeping particulars of transit money on the client file to which the transit money relates, will have to ensure that those particulars comply with cl 81.

Trust money subject to a power

Where the trust money received by a law practice is to be dealt with under a power to receive or disburse money for or on behalf of another person exercisable jointly and severally with the other person or a nominee of the other person, there is no need to deposit this money to the general trust account (s 254(1)). If the money is received in the form of cash however, s 258A(5) requires this money to be placed in the general trust account of the law practice (or a controlled money account in the case of controlled money), before dealing with it in accordance with the power.

Section 258 provides:

1 Subject to s 258A, a law practice that exercises a power to deal with trust money must deal with the money only in accordance with the power relating to the money.

2 The law practice must account for the money as required by the regulations.

In cl 85 LPR subsection 2 provides:

2 If a law practice or an associate of the law practice is given a power to deal with trust money (whether alone or jointly with another person), the practice must keep:

(a) a record of all dealings with the money to which the practice or associate is a party; and

(b) all supporting information in relation to the dealings, in a manner that enables the dealings to be clearly understood.

3 The record, supporting information, and power must be kept by the law practice as part of the practice's trust records.

In cl 86 (LPR) we find that a law practice must maintain a register of powers and estates in respect of which the law practice or an associate of the practice is acting or entitled to act, alone or jointly with the law practice or one or more associates of the practice, in relation to trust money. Where the power requires the law practice or associate to act jointly with another person(s) then there is no need to include this power in the register. The information to be included in the register of powers and estates is the name and address of the donor and date of each power and the name and date of death of the deceased in respect of each estate of which the law practice or associate is executor or administrator.

Notification requirements regarding general trust accounts – cl 74

A law practice establishing a general trust account after 1 October 2005 must give written notice of that fact within 14 days to the Law Society Council.

Within 14 days after the closure of a general trust account, a law practice must give written notice to the Law Society Council.

A law practice is required by cl 74(4) to give written notice to the Law Society Council

(a) either before, or within 14 days after, authorizing or terminating the authority of an associate of the practice or an Australian legal practitioner:
   (i) to sign cheques drawn on a general trust account of the practice; or
   (ii) otherwise to effect, direct or give authority for the withdrawal of money from a general trust account of the practice.
(b) during July of each year, must give the Law Society Council written notice of the associates and Australian legal practitioners (including their names and addresses) who are authorized, as at 1 July of that year:
   (i) to sign cheques drawn on the general trust account of the practice; or
   (ii) otherwise to effect, direct or give authority for the withdrawal of money from a general trust account of the practice.

Withdrawals from trust

When making payments from the trust account, a law practice must ensure that once trust money has been received it must be held for those beneficially entitled to it. The law practice must deal with that money, subject to the provisions of the legislation, pursuant to the directions of the client. In the case of *Adams v Bank of New South Wales* ([1984] 1 NSWLR 285, pp 290–92), Moffat P addressed the situation where a solicitor holds funds on behalf of a trustee:

> ... if a solicitor suspects that upon the money being paid to the client, he will apply some or all of it for purposes inconsistent with the client's duty as trustee... no ground arises for the solicitor to refuse to perform his obligation as solicitor and pay the money as directed by his client. He might refuse to act further for his client, but he could not refuse to pay the money as directed by his client.

Deficiency in trust account

Section 262 provides:

1 An Australian legal practitioner is guilty of an offence if he or she, without reasonable excuse, causes:
   (a) a deficiency in any trust account or trust ledger account; or
   (b) a failure to pay or deliver any trust money.
2 A reference in subsection (1) to an account includes a reference to an account of the practitioner or of the law practice of which the practitioner is an associate.

(3) In this section

(a) "cause" includes be responsible for.

(b) "deficiency" in a trust account or trust ledger includes the non-inclusion or exclusion of the whole or any part of an amount that is required to be included in the account.

Wilful contravention

There may be times when a practitioner is in breach of the legal accounting requirements due to a simple mistake. If, upon discovering the mistake, the practitioner takes immediate steps to remedy the situation, it is suggested that, on those occasions, the conduct of the solicitor would not be found to be professional misconduct.

Per Mr Justice Hardie in *Re Hodgekiss* ((1962) SR NSW 340, p 353) in relation to earlier legislation:

> The section deals with personal breaches of the statutory provisions in question on occasions when the solicitor knew or believed that he was committing such breaches, or was recklessly careless in that regard.

Mr Justice Hardie went on to say that it was essential to examine the facts and circumstances relevant to the solicitor's state of mind, knowledge, and intention at the material times. To determine whether a solicitor is guilty of professional misconduct, all of these factors will have to be taken into consideration.

A solicitor cannot delegate responsibility for the proper maintaining of the trust account. The Solicitors' Statutory Committee on the matter of Paul Vincent Wakim, reported in the supplement to the Law Society Journal August 1988, said:

> The importance of a solicitor's personal involvement in the supervision of his trust account is well illustrated by the fact that, had the solicitor in the present case been so involved and made regular inspections of the bank reconciliation statements prepared by his accountant, he would have detected at an early stage the deficiency created by the wrongful deposit. That he did not involve himself in such personal supervision amounted to the sort of reckless carelessness referred to by Hardie J in *Re Hodgekiss*.

Neither can a solicitor abandon his/her obligations to a partner or employee of the firm. In *Re Mayes and the Legal Practitioners Act 1974* (1 NSWLR 19), Reynolds JA and Hutley JA stated, p 25:

> It is no answer for the appellant to claim that he left the conduct of the financial affairs of the firm to his partner ... The existence of a system cannot relieve partners from personal vigilance.

Fit and proper person

In order to remain on the roll of persons admitted as lawyers, maintained by the Supreme Court, a practitioner must comply with his/her professional duty. A vital part of that duty is to comply with accounting obligations. As Street CJ stated in *Law Society of NSW v Jones* (1978, unreported, 27 July, NSWCA, p 10):

> Reliability and integrity in the handling of trust funds are fundamental prerequisites in determining whether an individual is a fit and proper person to be entrusted with the responsibilities belonging to a solicitor.

The courts must protect members of the public who place their trust in their solicitor. In the matter of *Law Society of New South Wales v Shenker* ([1999] NSWADT 37), the Tribunal made clear that its jurisdiction was protective and not punitive. The Tribunal referred to the judgement of Sheller JA in *Law Society of New South Wales v Bannister* (1993) 4 LPDR 24 at p 28:

> When the jurisdiction of the Tribunal is invoked under Pt 10, Division 7 of the Act to conduct a hearing into a complaint of professional misconduct by a legal practitioner, the primary consideration is to protect the public by preventing a person unfit to practice from holding himself or herself out to the public as a legal practitioner in who members of the public might repose confidence. The Tribunal must also act so as to deter the offender in the future and any other practitioner minded to behave in like manner.

Duty to report irregularity

In s 263 of the LPA we find that as soon as possible after a legal practitioner associate of a law practice becomes aware that there is an irregularity in any of the practice's trust accounts or trust ledger accounts, the associate must give written notice of the irregularity to the Law Society Council and any corresponding authority.

This duty is extended to apply in the situation where an Australian legal practitioner believes on reasonable grounds that there is an irregularity in connection with the receipt, recording, or disbursement of any trust money received by a law practice of which the practitioner is not a legal practitioner associate, the practitioner must, as soon as practicable after forming the belief, give written notice of it to the Law Society Council and any corresponding authority.

The section provides protection in s 263(3) to the extent that an Australian legal practitioner is not liable for any loss or damage suffered by another person as a result of the practitioner's compliance with the section.

2 Legal Costs

The amount which a law practice is able to charge a client for legal costs is governed by a number of factors. These include the fiduciary nature of the relationship between solicitor and client, market forces and legislative provisions. Prior to the commencement of the previous legislation, costs were regulated, in most cases, by scale. Except in those few areas of law where scale costs apply, legal costs are a matter of agreement between the law practice and the client.

Costs disclosure

Disclosure of legal costs and other matters is required by the Legal Profession Act 2004. Part 3.2 of the Act contains the provisions relating to costs disclosure and assessment. The obligation to disclose legal costs had been introduced to the legal profession with the commencement of the Legal Profession Reform Act 1993 and so this is not a new concept to law practices in New South Wales. Section 309 provides that a law practice must disclose to a client or prospective client the following:

(a) the basis of the calculation of costs, including whether scales apply,

(b) the client's right to

  (i) negotiate a costs agreement,

  (ii) receive a bill from the law practice, and

  (iii) request an itemised bill within 30 days after receipt of a lump sum bill and to be notified under s 316 of any substantial change to matters disclosed.

(c) an estimate of costs or if not possible a range,

(d) billing arrangements,

(e) rate of interest charged on overdue legal costs,

(f) in litigious matters, an estimate of the range of costs if the client is successful and the range of costs if the client is unsuccessful,

(g) the client's right to progress reports,

(h) person to contact to discuss legal costs,

(i) right to dispute costs by costs assessment, or by application to set aside costs agreement or by mediation,

(j) time limits,

(k) the jurisdiction which will apply to legal costs,

(l) the client must be informed that they have rights to sign an agreement or give notice that the corresponding law of another jurisdiction is to apply in relation to the matter.

In litigious matters it is further required that the law practice disclose that a costs order of the court may not cover the total of the client's legal costs and where applicable, that a client may be required to pay disbursements even where they entered into a conditional costs agreement. Section 310 deals with the requirements for disclosure where another law practice is to be retained.

Disclosure under s 309 must be made in writing before, or as soon as practicable after, the law practice is retained.

The disclosure must be in clear plain language and may be in a language other than English if the client is more familiar with that language. If the law practice is aware that the client is unable to read, it must arrange for the information to be conveyed orally to the client in addition to providing the written disclosure (s 315).

The Law Society of New South Wales has published a model costs disclosure form on its website.

There are some circumstances in which a law practice is not required to disclose in accordance with s 309 and 310.The exceptions are listed in s 312:

(a) costs, excluding disbursements, are unlikely to exceed $750 or an amount prescribed by the regulations (whichever is higher);
(b) if the client received one or more bills under s 309 or s 310(1) from the practice in the previous 12 months, the client has agreed in writing to waive the right to disclosure and the principal of the practice decides on reasonable grounds that further disclosure is not warranted. A written record of the principal's decision must be kept;
(c) the client is a practice or Australian legal practitioner, a public or foreign company or their subsidiary, a financial services licensee or a Minister of the Crown acting in that capacity;
(d) the costs or basis on which they will be calculated were agreed upon as part of a tender process;
(e) the client will not be required to pay the legal costs (such as in pro bono matters);
(f) in any circumstances prescribed by the regulations.

Additional disclosure is required where a practice negotiates a settlement of a litigious matter (s 313) and where the costs agreement includes an uplift fee (s 314).

A law practice has an obligation to notify the client of any substantial change to anything requiring disclosure under Division 3 (s 316).

Section 318(1) provides that on the reasonable request of the client, the practice must prepare a written report of the progress of the matter and a written report of the legal costs incurred by the client to date, or since the last bill (if any), in the matter. A law practice may charge for the preparation of the progress report relating to the matter but must not charge in relation to the progress report relating to costs.

The effect of failure to disclose anything required by Division 3 is set out in s 317. Where disclosure has not been made the client need not pay the legal costs unless they have been assessed; the client may apply under s 328 for the costs agreement to be set aside and the practice may not maintain proceedings for the recovery of costs until they have been assessed. Failure to comply is capable of being unsatisfactory conduct or professional misconduct.

Section 319 sets out when costs can be recovered. Costs are recoverable in accordance with a fixed costs provision, under a costs agreement made in accordance with Division 5 or otherwise according to the fair and reasonable value of the legal services provided. Costs are not recoverable for the making of disclosures required under Division 3.

Note that as 'legal costs' are defined in s 3 of the LPA to include disbursements, all disbursements must also be disclosed.

Where the matter is in relation to a personal injury damages claim within the meaning of the Civil Liability Act 2002 there are special requirements for disclosure. Division 9, 'Maximum costs in personal injury damages matters' and Division 10 'Costs in civil claims where no reasonable prospects of success', place further obligations on practitioners as a consequence of the Civil Liabilities Act 2002.

A number of decisions in the Family Court have highlighted its exclusive jurisdiction as to costs. The Family Court Rules 2004 in Chapter 19, set out the requirements for costs disclosure in that jurisdiction. The Family Court has exclusive jurisdiction to determine costs disputes between solicitor and client in relation to Family Court proceedings.

Costs agreements

Although disclosure of costs and estimates is mandatory, costs agreements are optional (s 322). A costs agreement must be in writing or evidenced in writing (s 322(2)). A disclosure document under the Legal Profession Act 2004 will not suffice as an offer in respect of a costs agreement. The Law Society of New South Wales has published model costs agreements on its website. According to s 322(5), a costs agreement cannot provide that the legal costs to which it relates are not subject to costs assessment. If a costs agreement contravenes or is entered into in contravention of, any provision of Division 3, it will be void (s 327).

A law practice may make a conditional costs agreement, in which the payment of the practice's costs is conditional upon the successful outcome of the matter (s 323 of the LPA). It must be in writing, in clear plain language and signed by the client. It must also contain a statement that the client has been informed of a right to seek independent legal advice before entering into the agreement and must specify that a five business days cooling-off period is available. The conditional costs agreement must set out the way in which a successful outcome will be determined. In the agreement, disbursements may be excluded from the costs that are payable only on the successful outcome of the matter. A conditional costs agreement may not be entered into in criminal proceedings or proceedings under the Family Law Act 1975 of the Commonwealth.

In s 324 (1) a law practice is prohibited from entering into a conditional costs agreement in relation to a claim for damages that provides for the payment of a premium on the legal costs payable under the agreement on the successful outcome of the matter. In other types of matters a conditional costs agreement may provide for the payment of a premium on those costs otherwise payable under the agreement. The premium must be a specified percentage of the legal costs (excluding unpaid disbursements) and must not exceed 25% of those costs (s 324(3) and (4)). If a practice enters into a costs agreement in contravention of this section it is liable to a fine of up to 100 penalty units.

Section 325 provides that the uplift is not to be contingent upon the value of any property or any transaction, or the amount of any award or settlement.

If a law practice enters into a costs agreement in contravention of either s 324 or 325, s 327 (4) provides that the practice is not to recover any costs in relation to the matter and must repay any amount received in respect of those services.

The New South Wales Administrative Tribunal considered a written costs agreement in *New South Wales Bar Association v Abdul-Karim (*2003 NSWADT 152). The agreement was to cover both criminal and civil proceedings. The agreement expressly provided that the barrister's hourly rate and court appearance charges would not apply and that he was to be remunerated by 20% of the amount recovered in the proposed civil proceedings. In the Tribunal's opinion the costs agreement was illegal as it breached s 186(3) of the LPA (now s 323(2)) because it was a conditional costs agreement entered into in respect of criminal proceedings. There was also a breach of s 188 LPA (now s 325) as the agreement provided that the barrister's fees were to be determined as 20% of the amount recovered in the civil proceedings covered by the agreement. The Tribunal stated:

> The prohibitions in the legislation are for the protection of the public in general and a specific client in particular. Nothing the Barrister has submitted could possibly justify his entering into such an agreement particularly in circumstances where he knew of the statutory prohibitions...The Barrister believed the charges would be dismissed and that in any event the potential damages would be very substantial. He agreed to a fee of 20%. As the applicant submitted there was present an element of unfair dealing and avarice involved.

The Tribunal found Ground 1 established and that the barrister's conduct amounted to professional misconduct.

Assessment of costs

In New South Wales, there are two systems that govern the recovery of legal costs. The more common system used is the assessment of costs as it governs all solicitor/client costs and most New South Wales jurisdictions for party/party costs. It is defined in the LPA and LPR. The second system is under the Federal taxation system.

Bills of costs in New South Wales jurisdictions are assessed by assessors appointed by the Supreme Court. The application is made to the Manager, Costs Assessment, at the Supreme Court. Either the client or the law practice can apply to have a bill assessed. The party applying for the assessment must pay the filing fee.

The circumstances in which a client may apply for an assessment of costs are set out in s 350. An application may be made even if the legal costs have been wholly or partly paid. If any costs have been paid without a bill, the client may still apply for a costs assessment. An application for assessment must be made within 60 days after the bill was given or the request was made or after the costs were paid in full, whichever is earliest.

An application by a law practice for costs assessment may not be made unless at least 30 days have passed since the bill was given or the request for payment was made (s 352).

Section 354 sets out how to make an application for costs assessment.

Written arguments are submitted to the assessor and neither party has the opportunity to present oral arguments or discuss their case. A costs assessor may require further particulars or documents to be provided (s 358). A legal practitioner who fails to comply with the request for further information under s 358 may be guilty of professional misconduct (s 358(4) of the LPA).

If an application for costs assessment is made where the disputed costs are subject to a costs agreement s 361 provides that the costs assessor must assess those costs by reference to the costs agreement where that agreement complies with Division 5 (costs agreements).

Criteria for assessment – s 363

1 In conducting an assessment of legal costs, the costs assessor must consider:
   - (a) whether or not it was reasonable to carry out the work to which the legal costs relate, and
   - (b) whether or not the work was carried out in a reasonable manner; and
   - (c) the fairness and reasonableness of the amount of legal costs in relation to the work.

2 In considering what is a fair and reasonable amount of legal costs the costs assessor may have regard to any or all of the following matters:

(a) whether the law practice and any Australian legal practitioner or Australian-registered foreign lawyer acting on its behalf complied with any relevant legislation or legal profession rules;

(b) any disclosures made by the law practice under Division 3 (costs disclosure), or the failure to make any disclosures required under that Division;

(c) any relevant advertisement as to

(i) the law practice's costs; or

(ii) the skills of the law practice or of any Australian legal practitioner or Australian-registered foreign lawyer acting on its behalf.

(d) any relevant costs agreement;

(e) the skill, labour, and responsibility displayed on the part of the Australian legal practitioner or Australian-registered foreign lawyer responsible for the matter;

(f) the retainer and whether the work done was within the scope of the retainer;

(g) the complexity, novelty, or difficulty of the matter;

(h) the quality of the work done;

(i) the place where, and circumstances in which, the legal services were provided;

(j) the time within which the work was required to be done;

(k) any other relevant matter.

Section 328 gives a costs assessor power to make an order setting aside a costs agreement if satisfied that the agreement is not fair and reasonable. In determining whether a costs agreement is fair and reasonable the costs assessor may have regard to:

(a) whether the client was induced to enter the agreement by fraud or misrepresentation;

(b) whether any Australian legal practitioner has been found guilty of unsatisfactory, professional conduct or professional misconduct in relation to any of the legal services;

(c) whether the law practice failed to make any of the disclosures required;

(d) the time at which the agreement was made.

Determination

Upon making a determination, a costs assessor issues each party a certificate of determination (s 368). The determination is final and binding.

On the filing of the certificate in the office or registry of a court having jurisdiction and with no further action, it is taken to be a judgement of that court for the amount of unpaid costs.

There is a procedure in s 373 of the LPA for the review of a costs assessor's determination. A dissatisfied party may, within 30 days after the issue of the certificate of determination, apply for a review to the Manager, Costs Assessment for a review of the determination. The initial determination is suspended until the review is completed.

Prior to the decision of the Court of Appeal in the case of *Attorney General (NSW) and Anor v Kennedy Miller Television Pty Ltd* ((1998) unreported, 30 June, CA40574/97), Masters of the Supreme Court of New South Wales had rejected the proposition that assessors had a duty to give reasons for their assessments. Since the *Kennedy Miller* case, a costs assessor has been required to give reasons when making a determination.

The requirement for a costs assessor to give reasons has now been enshrined in s 370 of the LPA

Costs fixed by regulation

According to s 329 of the LPA, costs for certain legal services may be fixed by regulation. The regulations may make provisions for:

(a) fixing fair and reasonable costs for legal services provided in any worker's compensation matter;

(b) fixing the costs payable for legal services provided in connection with any claim for personal injury damages (within the meaning of the Civil Liability Act 2002);

(c) fixing the costs payable for the enforcement of a lump sum debt or liquidated sum for damages;

(d) fixing the costs payable for the enforcement of a judgement by a judgement creditor;

(e) fixing the costs payable for legal services provided in respect of probate or the administration of estates;

(f) fixing an amount of costs for a matter that is not a legal service but is related to proceedings (for example, expenses for witnesses).

A legal practitioner cannot be paid or recover for a legal service any amount that exceeds the fair and reasonable cost fixed for the service by the regulations under s 329.

Overcharging

If, on a costs assessment or review, the costs assessor considers that the legal costs charged are grossly excessive, s 393 provides that the costs assessor must refer the matter to the Legal Services Commissioner to consider whether disciplinary action should be taken. Section 393(2) provides that a costs assessor must refer any other matter that may amount to unsatisfactory professional conduct or professional misconduct to the Commissioner.

Overcharging as grounds for a finding of professional misconduct was considered in the case of *New South Wales Bar Association v Amor-Smith* (2003) NSWADT 239. In all of the information laid by the New South Wales Bar Association it was alleged that the barrister was guilty of professional misconduct and/or unsatisfactory professional conduct. Count 2 related to overcharging and overservicing. It was alleged the barrister undertook unnecessary work, spent unreasonably long periods of time undertaking work, and improperly charged for matters. The decision of the Tribunal referred to the earlier cases of *Veghelyi v The Law Society of New South Wales*, Unreported, Court of Appeal, NSW, 6 October 1995 (BC950549) and *Law Society of New South Wales v Foreman* (1994) 34 NSWLR 408 which had indicated that an important factor in determining whether gross overcharging should be held to be professional misconduct is whether the client(s) involved should be characterised as 'vulnerable' and, if so, whether or not the practitioner knew or should have known this. In the *Amor-Smith* case the Tribunal found that the Barrister knew, or should have known, that the clients were vulnerable, in both senses of that word. The Tribunal was satisfied that the barrister was guilty of professional misconduct.

Federal Court

All party/party costs in Federal jurisdictions are governed by taxation. On taxation, bills of costs must be prepared on scale (an exception is where there is a costs agreement in a Family Court matter, specifying an hourly rate which is higher than the scale). Party/party costs on taxation are allowed on the basis of 'necessary or proper'.

The necessary or proper test is a much narrower test than the fair and reasonable test. Party/party costs do not always include items which the profession generally would consider as reasonable. When preparing for a federal taxation, you must draw an itemised bill of costs on the relevant Federal Court scale. The bill is then served on the Costs Respondent and filed in the Federal Court. The parties' representatives attend the taxation and are able to make oral submissions as to why a particular costs item should or should not be allowed.

Party/party costs

It is difficult to give a good answer to the question of what is a party/party cost. Party/party costs are awarded by the Court. In general, 'costs follow the event'. This means that the unsuccessful party must pay the successful party's costs.

Party/party costs are defined in the New South Wales Supreme Court Rules (Pt 52, r 23) as:

> On a taxation on a party and party basis, there shall be allowed all such costs as were necessary or proper for the attainment of justice or for enforcing or defending the rights of the party whose costs are being taxed.

On the other hand, regarding solicitor/client costs:

> . . . costs shall not be allowed insofar as they are unreasonably incurred, unless incurred with the approval of the client. (See (NSW) SCR Pt 52, Div 5, r 33.)

Most solicitors would argue that all their work is necessary or proper, yet it is still reduced on party/party taxation. Solicitors and clients must be aware that some work, even if practically necessary, will never be able to be claimed on a party/party basis.

'Indemnity costs' entitle a party to recover all of its costs incurred, usually from a certain date specified by the court. This date would be the date on which an offer of compromise was rejected.

3 The General Trust Account

The Legal Profession Regulation 2005 regulates many aspects of legal practice. It covers topics such as the admission of local lawyers, legal practice by Australian legal practitioners and by foreign lawyers, advertising, statutory deposits, costs disclosure, and assessment. Part 8, headed trust money and trust accounts, is that part of the Legal Profession Regulation 2005 which deals with the trust account and it is on this Part that we now focus.

General matters

In Division 1 we are provided with a description of the trust money to which Part 3.1 of the Act applies. We find in cl 53 that Part 8 of the LPR has effect for the purposes of Part 3.1 of the Act and accordingly applies to a law practice in respect of:

(a) trust money received by the practice in this jurisdiction, unless the practice has an office in one or more jurisdictions but not in this jurisdiction; and

(b) trust money received by the practice in another jurisdiction, if the practice has an office in this jurisdiction but in no other jurisdiction; and

(c) trust money received by the practice in another jurisdiction, if the practice has an office in

   (i) this jurisdiction; and

   (ii) one or more other jurisdictions, but not in the jurisdiction in which the money was received,

   unless the money is dealt with in accordance with the corresponding law of a jurisdiction in which the practice has an office.

The definitions section is found in cl 54.

Computerized accounting systems – cl 55 – 59

Any trust accounting records maintained on a computerised accounting system must comply with Division 2. Clause 56 requires that a paper copy of certain trust records must be printed. Trust account cash books are to be printed monthly, unless a copy of the books as at the end of the month is retained in electronic form that is readable or reportable on demand. The electronic copy must be retained by the law practice. Reconciliation statements, trust ledger trial balances, and lists of controlled money accounts and their balances are to be printed monthly at the end of each month. Trust ledger accounts, the register of controlled money, and the trust account transfer journal are to be printed before they are archived or deleted from the system. Where the clause requires a print out at the end of the month, the law practice must print out these records within 15 days of the end of the month.

It is a requirement of cl 57 that the law practice maintain a chronological record of the creation, amendment, or deletion of information in its computerised accounting system. In cl 58 further requirements are set out including ensuring that the system is not capable of deleting a trust ledger account unless the balance of the account is zero and all outstanding cheques have been presented. When an account is deleted, a copy of the account must be retained in permanent form.

Clause 59 provides that the law practice must ensure that a backup copy of all records required by Part 8 is made not less frequently than once each month. The backup copy must be retained and a complete set of backup copies must be kept in a separate location.

General trust accounts – cl 60

If a law practice does not have a general trust account it must, as soon as practicable after receiving trust money, establish a general trust account that satisfies the LPR. Clause 60 (2) sets out the requirements. A general trust account satisfies this clause if the account is established with an ADI. An ADI means an authorised deposit taking institution within the meaning of the Banking Act 1959 of the Commonwealth. The account is to be maintained in the jurisdiction. There are special provisions in relation to the name of the account. The name of the account is to include the name of the law practice or the business name under which the law practice engages in legal practice and is to include the expression 'law practice trust account' or 'law practice trust a/c'. The terms 'law practice' do not need to be repeated if those words form part of the name of the business. Where a law practice established a general trust account before 1 October 2005 it does not need to change the name of the account to include the expression 'law practice trust account'.

Trust account statements – cl 82

A trust account statement provides the client with a history of the matter and shows the balance, if any, remaining to the credit of the client's ledger. Clause 82 of the LPR requires a law practice to give a trust account statement to each person for whom or on whose behalf trust money is held or controlled by the law practice or an associate of the practice. A separate statement must be furnished for each trust ledger account. Where the practice maintains a record of controlled money, the practice must furnish a separate statement for each record. In the case of trust money subject to a power in respect of which the practice is to keep a record of all dealings with the money to which the practice or associate is a party, the practice must furnish a separate statement for each record.

In cl 82(5) we find the particulars required in a trust statement:

(a) all of the information required to be kept under this Part in relation to the trust money included in the relevant ledger account or record; and

(b) the remaining balance (if any) of the money.

A trust account statement looks just like the trust or controlled money ledger.

Clause 82(6) sets out when a trust account statement is to be furnished:

(a) on completion of the matter to which it relates;

(b) on reasonable request by the person for whom or on whose request the money is held or controlled;

(c) after 30 June in each year.

It is to be provided as soon as practicable after any of the above events.

Trust account statements are not required at the end of June if:

(a) the account is less than six months old; or

(b) the balance of the account is zero and no transaction affecting the account has taken place within the previous 12 months; or

(c) a trust account statement has been furnished within the last preceding 12 months and there has been no subsequent transaction affecting the ledger account or record.

The law practice must retain a copy of each trust account statement.

If an institutional client directs the law practice not to provide trust account statements under cl 82, the law practice is not required to do so (cl 83).

There is an example of a trust account statement in the specimen accounts.

Register of investments – cl 84

This clause applies if trust money referred to in s 244(3) of the Act is invested by a law practice for or on behalf of a client.

Intermixing money – cl 87

Section 260 of the Act provides that a law practice must not, otherwise than as allowed by the regulations, mix trust money with other money. Clause 87 allows a law practice to mix trust money with other money to the extent authorised by the Law Society Council and in accordance with any conditions imposed by that Council in relation to authorisation.

Withdrawing trust money for legal costs – cl 88

This clause prescribes the procedures to be followed for the withdrawal of trust money held in a general trust account or controlled money account for payment of legal costs owing to the practice by the person for whom the trust money was paid into the account to comply with s 261(1)(b) of the Act. The procedures are discussed later in the text.

Keeping of trust records – cl 89

Clause 89 has effect for the purposes of s 264 of the Act for the keeping in a permanent form of a law practice's trust records. Trust records are to be kept for a period of seven years after the last transaction entry in the record (cl. 89 (2)).This clause does not apply to a written direction referred to in s 254(1)(a) or 256 of the Act.

Retaining other records and information – cl 90

Any record or information required to be maintained by Part 8 of the Regulation is to be kept for seven years after the finalisation of the matter to which the record relates.

Statements regarding receipt or holding of trust money – cl 91

The Law Society Council may require a law practice to provide to it a statement specifying that the law practice has received or held trust money during a period specified by the council. The law practice must specify the category of trust money received or held.

4 Primary Accounting Records

Trust receipts – cl 61

The trust receipt is the source document which records the receipt of trust money. It is from this source document that the cash receipts book is written up and then posted to the ledger. It is vital that the information on the receipt is correct in all respects, so that subsequent entries and postings are also correct. When a law practice receives trust money that is required to be paid into a general trust account then, as soon as practicable after receiving trust money, the law practice must make out or cause to be made out a receipt in duplicate which contains all the particulars as set out in subclause 5:

- the date the receipt is made out and, if different, the date of receipt of money;
- the amount of money received;
- the form in which it is received (cheque, cash, or direct deposit);
- the name of the person from whom the money was received;
- details identifying the name of the client in respect of whom the money was received and the matter description and matter reference;
- particulars sufficient to identify the purpose for which the money was received;
- the name of the law practice or the business name under which the law practice engages in legal practice and the expression 'trust account' or 'trust a/c';
- be consecutively numbered in series;
- the name of the person who made out the receipt;
- the number of the receipt.

A solicitor must issue receipts in the numerical order of the series to which they belong (cl 61(7)). The original of the receipt is to be delivered, on request, to the person from whom the trust money is received (cl 61(6)). If a receipt is cancelled or not delivered, the original receipt must be retained.

Where the trust money is received by direct deposit, the law practice is required to make out a receipt as soon as practicable after the practice receives or can access notice or confirmation (in written or electronic form) of the deposit from the ADI concerned.

This receipt, if completed in accordance with the Regulation, will comply. A completed receipt can be found in the specimen accounts.

Receipt No.:

Date:_______________

TRUST ACCOUNT RECEIPT

Received From ____

On ____________________________________

the sum of ____

$ _______________________________________ Cheque/Cash/Direct Deposit

For and on behalf of:

____

Reason: ____

____

Received by: ______________________

On behalf of:

Law Practice

Multi-receipt

From time to time, a client will give a solicitor one cheque (or cash) which covers a number of matters. The solicitor may issue one receipt which covers all matters. This is often referred to as a multi-receipt. The multi-receipt must detail the exact amount which is to be credited to each matter.

Bank card

A solicitor may apply to operate as a merchant for credit card purposes. A credit card voucher may be acceptable trust funds and deposited into the trust account. The credit card must be of the type that permits the whole transaction amount to be credited to the trust account. Any fees associated with the transaction must not be debited to the trust account.

Dishonoured cheque

When the dishonour of a cheque which has been banked into your trust account occurs, the following procedure should be followed:

1 file the notification from the bank in the appropriate file;
2 record the dishonour in the cash receipts, including the reason for the reversal and entering the amount of the cheque as a negative amount;
3 post the entry to the debit side of the ledger;
4 where the dishonoured amount has been drawn against (this should not occur as any funds dealt with in the trust account must be cleared funds),

then a deposit must be made from the office account to the trust account. A receipt is issued in the usual way, an entry made in the cash book and then posted to the credit side of the ledger;

5 check that the bank does not debit the dishonour fee from your trust account. The dishonour fee must be debited to your office account.

Cancelled receipts

From time to time, you will need to cancel a receipt. A receipt must not be cancelled unless the original receipt has been retained. Clause 61(8) provides that the solicitor must retain any original receipt that is cancelled after issue. The most common reason for cancelling a trust receipt would probably be where a receipt was made out for trust when the money is due to the office account.

When cancelling a receipt:

1 keep the cancelled receipt in the receipt book;

2 write across the receipt and duplicate 'cancelled';

3 record the receipt number in the cashbook and write 'cancelled' next to it. This will keep the receipt numbers in consecutive order. No posting to the ledger;

4 the reason for the cancellation should be noted on the receipt and in the cashbook.

Bank deposits – cl 62

The bank deposit slip is the source document which provides evidence of the deposit of receipts of trust money into the trust bank account.

Clause 62 applies when a law practice receives trust money that is required to be paid into a general trust account otherwise than by a direct deposit. A deposit record must be produced to the approved ADI at the time the deposit is made. The following particulars must be recorded on the deposit record:

(a) the date of the deposit;

(b) the amount of the deposit;

(c) whether the deposit is in the form of cheques, notes, or coins (and the amount of each);

(d) the details of each cheque, including the name of the drawer, the bank and branch (or BSB number) of the ADI, and the amount.

A duplicate of the deposit record is retained in the solicitor's bank deposit book. The bank teller should stamp and initial the duplicate deposit record. A bank deposit record is not required in the case of money credited directly to a bank account, electronically or otherwise. A solicitor must, of course, check that any funds deposited in this way have been received by the bank before drawing on those funds.

This deposit slip will comply with the Regulation if completed correctly. A completed deposit slip can be found in the specimen accounts.

UTS BANK

Credit Listing

Drawer	Bank	Branch or BSB Number	Amout
1			
2			
3			
4			
5			
6			
7			
8			

Deposit date

CSO tellers – initials

Cheques

Trading date

State Cr Tax

cash

Account name

Cash breakup

$100	$______	00
$50	$______	00
$20	$______	00
$10	$______	00
$5	$______	00
Coin	$______	00
Total	$______	__
Change	______	__
Total Cash	$______	__

Total

$ ______

Total

$ ______

Total to Credit Summary

$ ______

BSB number

Account Number

Cheques in this deposit are not availabe until cleared

Manner of withdrawal of trust money – cl 64

Clause 64 sets out the manner in which trust money may be withdrawn from a general trust account. Trust money may be withdrawn by cheque in accordance with cl 65 or by electronic funds transfer in accordance with c/66. Cash withdrawals, ATM withdrawals or transfers, and telephone banking withdrawals or transfers are specifically prohibited.

Payment by cheque – cl 65

To comply with the Regulation, a cheque must:

- be made payable to or to the order of a specified person or persons and not to bearer or cash; and
- be crossed 'not negotiable'; and
- include the name of the law practice or the business name under which the law practice engages in legal practice and the expression 'law practice trust account' or 'law practice trust a/c'.

The requirement to have the words 'law practice' on each cheque does not apply to those law practices with an account established in this jurisdiction before 1 October 2005. If the words 'law practice' form part of the name or business name of the law practice there is no need to repeat that expression.

A cheque must be signed by an authorised principal of the law practice or if a principal is not available then by an authorised legal practitioner associate or by an authorised Australian legal practitioner who holds an unrestricted practicing certificate authorising the receipt of trust money or by two or more associates jointly.

In cl 65 the term 'associate' means an associate of the law practice. 'Authorised' means authorised by the law practice to sign cheques drawn on the trust account.

A written record of the required particulars must be kept of each payment by cheque. Usually this will be in the form of a cheque butt. The required particulars are:

- the date and number of the cheque;
- the amount of the payment;
- the name of the person to whom the payment is to be made or in the case of a cheque made payable to an ADI, the name of the ADI and the name of the person receiving the benefit of the payment;
- details clearly identifying the ledger account to be debited;
- detail clearly identifying the name of the person on whose behalf the cheque is drawn and the matter reference;
- reason for the payment.

Written records relating to payments by cheque (including cheque requisitions) must be stored in the order in which the cheques were issued.

Electronic funds transfer – cl 66

The only alternative to withdrawing trust money by cheque is by way of an electronic funds transfer. Clause 66 sets out the way the transfer is to be carried out.

An electronic funds transfer is to be effected by, or under the direction, or with the authority of:

- an authorised principal of the law practice; or
- if an authorised principal is not available then an authorised Australian legal practitioner associate; or
- an authorised Australian legal practitioner who holds an unrestricted practising certificate authorising the receipt of trust money; or
- two or more authorised associates jointly.

In cl 66 'associate' means an associate of the law practice and 'authorised' means authorised by the law practice to effect, direct, or give authority for an electronic funds transfer from the general trust account.

For each electronic funds transfer the following particulars are required to be kept:

- the date and number of the transaction;
- the amount transferred;
- the name and number of the account to which the amount was transferred and relevant BSB number;
- the name of the person to whom the payment was made or, in the case of a payment to an ADI, the name or BSB number of the ADI and the name of the person receiving the benefit of the payment;
- details clearly identifying the name of the person on whose behalf the payment was made and the matter reference;
- the details clearly identifying the ledger account to be debited;
- particulars sufficient to identify the purpose for which the payment was made.

Written records relating to payments by electronic funds transfer must be stored in the order in which the transfers were effected.

Funds must be available

Before a trust cheque is drawn, a check must be made to ensure that the funds in that particular ledger account have been cleared. This means the law practice must wait for the number of days that the bank has advised it will take a cheque to clear before drawing on that cheque.

If a practitioner needs to use funds provided by a client by way of a personal cheque, a special clearance of that cheque can be arranged on payment of a fee. The bank will then notify the practitioner when that cheque has been cleared and the funds are available to draw on. Clients are not always aware that personal cheques deposited into trust will take several days to clear. You should advise your clients of this or request that the money to be paid into trust be by way of a bank cheque (note, however, that bank cheques also take several days to clear).

Practitioners should always sight supporting documentation (and initial it so that it cannot be used a second time) when signing cheques. It is essential that the firm has the authority to make the payment.

Who can sign a trust account cheque or effect an electronic funds transfer?

In cl 65(3) we find that a cheque must be signed by an authorised principal of the law practice or if a principal is not available then by an authorised legal practitioner associate or by an authorised Australian legal practitioner who holds an unrestricted practising certificate authorising the receipt of trust money. A further alternative is by two or more authorised associates signing jointly. The same parties may be authorised to effect an electronic funds transfer. If a principal of a law practice is not available then other persons such as an employed legal practitioner, a legal practitioner with an unrestricted practicising certificate, and an employee of the law practice may operate the general trust account provided they are authorised by the law practice. The requirement that a law practice must seek permission to authorise persons to sign trust cheques or effect electronic funds transfers has not been included in the Legal Profession Regulation 2005. A law practice must notify the Law Society in writing before or within 14 days after authorising or terminating the authority of an associate or an Australian legal practitioner to effect, direct, or give authority for the withdrawal of money from a general trust account (Cl 74).

A law practice is further required to give the Law Society during July written notice of the associates or Australian legal practitioners who are authorised to sign trust cheques or effect electronic funds transfers.

Multi-cheque

From time to time, a practitioner will need to draw a cheque with one payee which covers a number of matters. The practitioner may draw one cheque which covers all matters. This is referred to as a multi-cheque. The cheque butt must detail the exact amount which is to be debited from each matter. A common example of the use of a multi-cheque is in the payment of costs and disbursements from the trust account to the office account.

How to cancel a cheque

It is possible to cancel a cheque in circumstances where the firm retains possession of the cheque.

The Investigation Department of the Law Society of New South Wales recommends the following procedure when cancelling a cheque:

(a) the cheque is to be crossed 'cancelled' and the signature torn from the cheque;
(b) the cheque butt/requisition is to be crossed 'cancelled' and the reason for the cancellation recorded;
(c) the original of the cheque is to be retained and the cancelled cheque stapled to the cheque butt/requisition;
(d) the entry is to be recorded in cheque number sequence in the cashbook with the notation reading 'cancelled', the reason for the cancellation, and a nil dollar value recorded;
(e) the entry is not posted to a ledger account under the manual accounting system.[1]

How to stop payment on a cheque

When a mistake is discovered after a cheque has been issued to a third party it will be necessary to stop payment on the cheque. The first step is to notify the third party to whom the cheque has been issued. The issuing bank will need to be contacted and requested to issue a stop payment order. It is necessary to enter the reversal of the cheque in the cashbook by rewriting the entry in the cashbook, including the reason for the reversal and recording the amount as a negative amount. This will cancel the original entry.

A posting will need to be made to the ledger, this time on the credit side, that is, on the opposite side to the posting for the cheque originally.

When is a cheque too old?

Section 3(5) of the Cheques Act 1986 (Commonwealth) provides that a cheque which has been drawn and not presented for 15 months becomes stale. It will not be processed. A law practice should review all unpresented cheques on a regular basis. Action should be taken in respect of any cheque which has not been presented for three months.

When a cheque becomes stale, the cheque should be stopped and the procedure set out in 'How to Stop Payment of a Cheque' should be followed.

Bank cheques

A bank cheque is a cheque drawn by a bank on itself. It is usually accepted in lieu of cash, but it is not the same as cash. When your bank issues a bank

1 Law Society of New South Wales, *Legal Accounting Handbook*, 2005, 5th edition, Sydney, p. 37.

cheque, the bank does not treat it as cleared funds. Bank cheques are signed by officers of the bank. In most cases a bank cheque must be signed by two officers of the bank.

How do you obtain a bank cheque with trust money?

If, for example, you have a settlement of a conveyancing matter and you need to purchase a bank cheque for $200,000.00 in favour of V Vendor with trust money, then there are two possible ways to do this:

1 draw a trust account cheque for $200,000.00 in favour of 'UTS Bank' (the bank where you have your trust money) and, on the back, write 'Please issue a bank cheque for $200,000.00 in favour of V Vendor'. You, as the principal authorised to operate the account signs here and on the front of the cheque; *or*

2 draw a trust account cheque in favour of 'UTS Bank for bank cheque in favour of V Vendor'.

Either way, UTS Bank will give you a cheque drawn by the bank for $200,000.00 in favour of V Vendor.

Note: the first method allows the use of one cheque to obtain a number of bank cheques as required. The second method involves using one trust cheque for each bank cheque with associated fees and duties.

The bank charges a fee for the issuing of the bank cheque. This fee should not come from the trust account, but, rather, the solicitor should arrange to have the bank cheque fee(s) debited from the solicitor's office account.

The book-keeping procedures for recording the drawing of the cheque are exactly the same as for any other trust account cheque: details recorded on the cheque butt, entered in the cash payments book and posted as a debit in the client's individual trust ledger. Note that where the cheque is in favour of an ADI, you must record on the cheque butt the name of the person receiving the benefit.

5 Secondary Accounting Records

So far we have looked at the primary accounting records of the trust system. Receipts, bank deposit records, cheques, cheque butts, and electronic funds transfer authorities make up the primary records.

Here is a diagram which shows the basic trust account system:

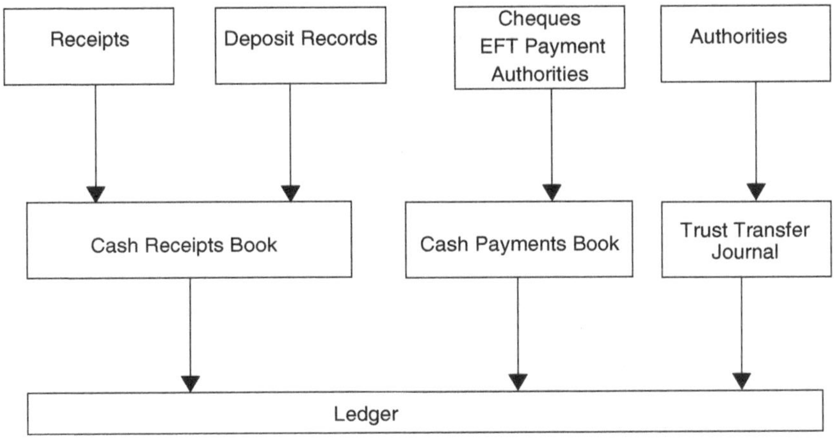

We now look at the secondary accounting records.

A law practice that maintains a general trust account is required by cl 67 LPR to maintain a trust account receipts cash book together with a trust account payments cash book. A cash book records the law practice's side of transactions which affect the cash in our bank account. It records the money coming into the trust account and the money leaving the trust account. It is a summary of receipt and payment transactions and is written up from the information on the receipts and cheque butts and electronic funds transfer authorities. The cash book is referred to as a book of first entry. It is the first time the information is written into an accounting book.

The format of the cash book may be decided by each firm so long as the information required is recorded. At the start of each new month a new page of the cash book should be commenced.

Trust account receipts cash book – cl 68

Clause 68 provides that the following particulars must be recorded in a law practice's trust account receipt cash book:

(a) the date a receipt was made out for the money and, if different, the date of receipt of the money;
(b) the receipt number;
(c) the amount of the money received;
(d) the form in which the money was received;
(e) the name of the person from whom the money was received;
(f) details clearly identifying the name of the client in respect of whom the money was received and the matter description and matter reference;
(g) particulars sufficient to identify the purpose for which the money was received;
(h) details clearly identifying the ledger account to be credited.

The particulars of a receipt must be recorded in the order in which the receipts are made out and must be entered in the cash book within five working days counting from and including the day the receipt was made out.

The date and amount of each deposit in the general trust account must be recorded in the trust account cash receipts book.

Trust account payments cash book – cl 69

Clause 69(1) provides that the following particulars must be recorded in a law practice's trust account payments cash book in respect of each payment of trust money by cheque:

(a) the date and number of the cheque;
(b) the amount ordered to be paid by the cheque;
(c) the name of the person to whom the payment is to be made or, in the case of a cheque made payable to an ADI, the name or BSB number of the ADI and the name of the person receiving the benefit of the payment;
(d) details clearly identifying the name of the person on whose behalf the payment was made and the matter reference;
(e) details clearly identifying the ledger account to be debited;
(f) particulars sufficient to identify the purpose for which the payment was made.

There are similar requirements in cl 69(2) in those situations where the law practice makes a payment of trust money by way of electronic funds transfer:

(a) the date and number of the transaction;
(b) the amount transferred;

(c) the name and number of the account to which the amount was transferred and the relevant BSB number;
(d) the name of the person to whom the payment was made or, in the case of a payment to an ADI, the name or BSB number of the ADI and the name of the person receiving the benefit of the payment;
(e) details clearly identifying the name of the person on whose behalf the payment was made and the matter reference;
(f) details clearly identifying the ledger account to be debited;
(g) particulars sufficient to identify the purpose for which the payment was made.

The particulars of payments must be recorded in the order in which the payments are made and must be entered in the cash book within five working days counting from and including the day the payment was made out.

The following format of the cash receipts book and the cash payments book will comply with the Regulation. Completed cash receipts book and cash payments book can be found in the specimen accounts.

The entries in the cash book must then be posted to (recorded in) the ledger.

Recording transactions in trust ledger accounts – cl 70

Clause 70 of the Legal Profession Regulation 2005 provides that a law practice must maintain a separate ledger account for each matter for each person for whom, or on whose behalf, trust money is held.

The ledger tells you how much money you are holding on behalf of each client in each matter. It is often referred to as a book of summary. The ledger is written up from the cash book or the journal. No posting should be made in the ledger until after the primary records and the entries in the cash book have been completed.

When posting to the ledger, the receipts are recorded in the credit column, while the payments are recorded in the debit column. The ledger also has a column that shows the progressive balance.

Each time a transaction is recorded, the balance must be adjusted. The client owns the money in the ledger, so the client is in credit to the solicitor. The balance shows how much the client is owed.

Each trust ledger for a client must have a credit balance or zero balance. If the client's ledger reveals a debit balance, then, unless the ledger has a mathematical error, there must have been a breach of s 255 of the LPA. That is, some other client's money must have been used to meet a payment drawn against the account.

In addition to a ledger for each matter a client has money in the trust account, there is a ledger for the Bank. This is the Bank Control Account. The total receipts and total payments for each month are recorded in this ledger.

Trust Account Receipts Cash Book

For Period / / to / / Page:

Date Rct/ Rec'd	Rec.No. Form	Received From: Purpose	Account Name, Matter Description and Matter Reference	Ledger A/c No.	Multi-Amount	Rec Amount	Banking Deposit Total	Date

Trust Account Payments Cash Book

For Period / / to / / Page:

Date	Cheque No.	Paid to: Purpose	Account Name, Matter Description and Matter Reference	Ledger A/c No.	Multi-Amount	Cheque Amount

The title of a trust ledger account is prescribed in cl 70(2). It must include:

(a) the name of the person for or on whose behalf the trust money is paid;
(b) the person's address;
(c) particulars sufficient to identify the matter in relation to which the trust money was received.

Details of any changes in the title of a trust ledger must be recorded.

Clause 70(4) sets out the detail that must be recorded on the ledger account in respect of each receipt of trust money for the matter:

(a) the date a receipt was made out for the money and, if different, the date of receipt of trust money;
(b) the receipt number;
(c) the amount of money received;
(d) the name of the person from whom the money was received;
(e) particulars sufficient to identify the purpose for which the money was received.

Clause 70(5) sets out the detail that must be recorded in the trust ledger account in respect of each payment of trust money by cheque:

(a) the date and number of the cheque;
(b) the amount ordered to be paid by the cheque;
(c) the name of the person to whom the payment is to be made or, in the case of a cheque made payable to an ADI, the name or BSB number of the ADI and the name of the person receiving the benefit of the payment;
(d) particulars sufficient to identify the purpose for which the payment was made.

Clause 70(6) sets out the detail that must be recorded in the trust ledger account in respect of each payment of trust money by electronic funds transfer:

(a) the date and number of the transaction;
(b) the amount transferred;
(c) the name and number of the account to which the amount was transferred and the relevant BSB number;
(d) the name of the person to whom the payment was made or, in the case of a payment to an ADI, the name or BSB number of the ADI and the name of the person receiving the benefit of the payment;
(e) particulars sufficient to identify the purpose for which the payment was made.

When a transfer of trust money is made by a journal entry then cl 70(7) provides the particulars to be recorded:

(a) the date of the transfer;
(b) the amount transferred;
(c) the journal reference number;

(d) the name of the other trust ledger account from which or to which the money was transferred;

(e) particulars sufficient to identify the purpose for which the payment was made.

Transactions relating to trust money must be recorded in the trust ledger account in the order in which the transactions occur.

The particulars in respect of a receipt, payment, or transfer of trust money must be recorded within five working days counting from and including the day the receipt was made out, the payment was made, or the transfer was effected, as the case requires.

This style of ledger will comply with the Regulation:

The ledger is the core of the book-keeping system. Each transaction results in a double entry, one entry being a debit and the other a credit, so that once both entries are recorded the balances of the ledger accounts are calculated from those entries; the total of all the debit balances should equal the total of all the credit balances.

The 'double entry system of book-keeping' is the principle upon which trust accounting is based. We are not making a study of the double entry theory of book-keeping here. However, you will need to remember that every transaction is posted twice to the ledger – once as a debit and once as a credit. For every debit, there is a corresponding credit, and for every credit, there is a corresponding debit.

Sometimes, an item is posted to one account now and the corresponding item is only posted at the end of the month as part of a total.

A simple way to determine whether a transaction involves a debit or a credit entry in the ledger is:

(a) where you have a cash book receipt – credit in the ledger (total receipts for the month will then be a debit in the Bank Control Account);

(b) where you have a cash book payment – debit in the ledger (total payments for the month will then be a credit in the Bank Control Account).

Trust ledger account in name of law practice or legal practitioner associate – cl 73

A law practice is not permitted to maintain a trust ledger account in its own name or the name of a legal practitioner associate of the practice except as authorised by cl 73. Clause 73 allows such accounts for two purposes:

(a) for aggregating in the account, by transfer from other trust ledgers, money which is properly due to the law practice for legal costs. It must be withdrawn not later than one month after the transfer;

(b) for money in which the legal practitioner associate has a personal and beneficial interest (such as a vendor, mortgagee, lessee, or other similar

TRUST ACCOUNT LEDGER

NAME: ____________________

ADDRESS: ____________________

____

LEDGER NO: ______________ DESCRIPTION : ____________________

OTHER PARTY : ____________________

SOLICITOR HANDLING: ______________ RESPONSIBLE PARTNER: ____________

For Period / / to / /

Date Rct Rec'd/Pd	Ref. No.	Rec'd From or Paid To Purpose	Debit Amount	Credit Amount	Balance

capacity). The money must be withdrawn at the conclusion of the matter to which it relates.

This Regulation superseded an earlier direction given by the Council of the Law Society following the decision of the Court of Appeal in *Johns'* case (*Johns v Law Society of New South Wales* (1982) 2 NSWLR 1). In that case, the Court of Appeal considered the propriety of the solicitor maintaining a personal account within the trust ledger system. The Court was of the view that a solicitor should not, as the solicitor cannot hold money on trust to which the solicitor is absolutely entitled. In such a situation, the trust account records do not disclose the true position in relation to the money received. The Court of Appeal made it clear that, on general law principles, a trustee should not mix the trustee's personal funds with the trust's funds.

In a later case, *Malfanti v Legal Profession Disciplinary Tribunal* (reported in the November 1993 supplement to the Law Society Journal), the Court of Appeal took a different view to that expressed in *Johns*' case. His Honour Mr Justice Clarke, in considering the propriety of having a ledger account containing a balance to cover unexpected debits to the trust account, said:

> I see nothing wrong with the solicitor maintaining an account in his own name in the trust account, provided, of course, that it is always in credit.

Of course, a solicitor may maintain a ledger account in the solicitor's name just for the purposes listed in cl 73.

False names in trust account

A law practice must not knowingly receive money or record receipt of money in the trust records under a false name. If a person is commonly known by more than one name then the practice must ensure that the practice's trust records show all names by which that person is known (s 265 LPA).

In the matter of *Cahill v The Law Society of New South Wales* (reported in the supplement to the Law Society Journal November 1988), the court considered the practice by the solicitor of maintaining accounts within the firm's trust account for clients in assumed names. The use of the pseudonym was to defraud the Department of Social Services. The solicitor was aware of this intention. The court found the solicitor's conduct to amount to professional misconduct.

Journal transfers – cl 72

In addition to the cash book, there is another book of first entry. That is the journal. No posting should appear in a client ledger unless the transaction has been recorded in a book of first entry. In the trust account, that must either be the trust cash book or the trust journal.

The trust account transfer journal is used to record all transactions which are effected without any receipts or payments from the trust account. It is a movement of funds from one ledger account to another. Clause 71 provides that trust money may be transferred by journal entry but only if the law practice is entitled to do so. The transfer must be authorised in writing by either a person who is authorised to sign cheques drawn on the general trust account or by two or more persons who are authorised to sign cheques drawn on the general trust account jointly. The authorisation for each transfer of trust money by journal entry must be kept either in the trust account transfer journal or in some other way.

A trust journal transaction does not alter the total balance of the firm's trust account in any way. One of the most common uses of the trust journal is to record the transfer of money from a sale matter to a purchase matter for the same client. It can also be used to correct an incorrect posting or where a cost clearing account is used by a law practice to aggregate costs due to the firm, in accordance with cl 73 of the Regulation.

If a law practice transfers trust money by journal entry then it must keep a trust account transfer journal. Clause 71(3) prescribes the particulars that must be recorded:

(a) the date of the transfer;

(b) the trust ledger account from which the money is transferred (including its identifying reference);

(c) the trust ledger account to which the money is transferred (including its identifying reference);

(d) the amount transferred;

(e) particulars sufficient to identify the purpose for which the transfer is made, the matter reference, and a short description of the matter.

This format of the journal will comply with the Regulation:

Examples of journal entries are in the specimen accounts.

To complete the 'Journal ref' column, the transaction number must be inserted. For example, the first internal transfer in the trust ledgers will be No 1. It is the same number for both the debit part of the transfer and the credit part of the transfer. The details of the ledger account from which the money is being transferred are recorded first. The amount is a debit. Next, the details of the ledger account to which the money is being transferred are recorded and the amount noted as a credit. Then, the purpose for the transfer is entered.

To complete the 'Account name/matter no/matter description/purpose', make sure you give full details of the matter and do not forget to record a full description of the purpose for the transfer.

The entries in the journal are then posted to the individual ledger accounts. This effects a debit to the ledger account from which the funds are being transferred, and a credit to the ledger account to which the money is being transferred.

TRUST ACCOUNT TRANSFER JOURNAL

Date	Journal Ref	Authorised By	Account Name, Matter Reference, Matter Description, Purpose	Ledger A/c No.	Debit Amount	Credit Amount

Of course, any transfer by way of the journal must be authorised by the person on whose behalf the money is being held. It is always best to obtain written authority from that person, although this is not strictly required.

Practice without a trust account

In those instances where a solicitor has determined not to maintain a general trust account, the solicitor must never receive money on trust from a client. Before the commencement of the Legal Profession Act 2004 it was possible for the practice to operate by requesting transit money from the client and delivering that money in accordance with the instructions received, within the prescribed time. Section 258A now places an obligation on the law practice, when transit money is received in the form of cash, to first deposit that money into the general trust account. Law practices may receive controlled money accounts without operating a general trust account.

Notwithstanding that a practice does not maintain a general trust account, the affairs of the practice may still be investigated by the Law Society. The power to investigate the affairs of solicitors is contained in Division 3 of Chapter 3 of the LPA.

6 The Office Account

In a law practice, in addition to the trust account, an office account is maintained. The office account is entirely separate from the trust account, as it must be, to reflect the duty of a fiduciary to keep the trustee's own money separate from the fiduciary's clients. The office account records the financial transactions of the business. Whereas the LPA 2004 and the LPR 2005 strictly regulate the way in which the trust account is operated, the way you operate your office account is up to you. No special regulations control it, except that you are under the same obligations that affect any business.

Section 262A of the Income Tax Assessment Act 1936 (Commonwealth) provides that every person carrying on a business shall keep sufficient records in English of income and expenditure to enable assessable income and allowable deductions to be readily ascertained. The records must be retained for at least seven years after the completion of the transactions to which they relate.

Further, GST (Goods and Services Tax) is payable on legal services unless it is a GST-free or input taxed supply. Consequently, the legal practitioner will be liable to pay GST. This liability must be recognised and recorded in the office account. By s 8L of the Taxation Administration Act 1953 (Commonwealth), a person is guilty of an offence where that person keeps records in such a way that they do not correctly record and explain the transactions to which they relate.

Apart from the legislative requirements to maintain an office account, it is important that the owners of a legal practice are able to monitor the financial progress of that practice.

The system which is outlined here is only one of many possible. We will apply the same stringent account keeping requirements as in the trust account. The setting out of the office records that we will be using in the transaction accounts for Potter and Associates is slightly different from those used in the trust account.

Primary accounting records

The primary records in the office account consist of:

- office receipts;
- office cheques and cheque butts;
- office bank deposit books;
- petty cash vouchers; and
- memoranda of costs and disbursements.

The first three are all familiar to us from the trust account and are completed in exactly the same way.

The final two are found in the office account only. We shall look at memoranda of costs and disbursements and petty cash vouchers when we examine the secondary records to which they relate.

Secondary records

The secondary records in the office account consist of:

- office cash book – one for receipts and one for payments;
- petty cash book;
- costs journal;
- office journal (or general journal).

The cash book in the office account is maintained in the same way as the cash book in the trust account. However, the office cash book has additional columns of information. These are to record necessary details for the GST.

Here is a diagram that shows the basic office account system:

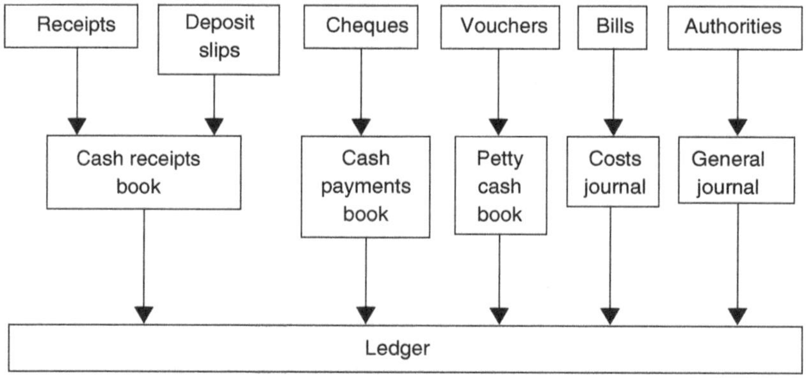

Petty cash book (or petty cash journal)

There are times when a purchase is too small for the use of a cheque or an organisation from which the firm is purchasing will not accept a cheque. In these instances, cash will have to be used to make the purchase. A common use of the money in petty cash is to buy coffee and biscuits to sustain the firm! The petty cash book acts as a record of these cash purchases and enables you to keep an eye on how much you are spending on these purchases. From the petty cash book, appropriate entries are posted to the office ledger.

To create 'petty cash', a cheque is drawn to 'cash'. This is often referred to as 'the float'. The cheque is cashed and the money placed in a security tin.

(It often helps to understand petty cash if you can visualise the tin with the money in it, so let's say the cheque is for $200. Visualise the $200 in the tin!)

The accounting procedures that must be followed when you draw that cheque to 'cash' for the float are:

1 draw the cheque;
2 complete the cheque butt;
3 record the drawing of the cheque in the office cash payments book;
4 post it to the ledger as a debit in the private ledger account petty cash;
5 record in the receipts column of the petty cash book.

When the money in the tin is used to make a purchase, the general practice is:

1 complete a petty cash voucher;
2 record the entry in the petty cash book including GST details;
3 post the entry in the ledger account showing the source as PC (petty cash), together with the page number of the petty cash book. This is posted as a debit.

Commonly, the writing up of the petty cash book does not occur on a daily basis. That is one of the reasons it is important that the primary record, the petty cash voucher, is completed each time money from petty cash is spent.

Here are the book-keeping entries where the float is $200 and $8.60 is spent purchasing coffee and tea.

Costs journal

In order to be paid for work which has been carried out on the instructions of a client, a law practice sends out a bill of costs to that client. The bill informs the client of the amount owing for costs and disbursements in a particular matter. The bill is the primary record from which the costs journal is written up. The costs journal is used to record all bills issued by the firm. It is only the costs (that is, the legal fees) component of the bill that is recorded in the costs journal. Disbursements are paid by cheque or out of petty cash so they appear in the ledger.

The procedure to be followed when sending a bill of costs is:

1 prepare the bill;
2 record the costs (that is the fee you have charged for your services) in the costs journal;
3 record the rendering of the costs in the client's ledger account as a debit to the client.

Here is a page of the costs journal after two entries :

1 On 2 February 20xx, you prepared a bill in accordance with your costs agreement in the matter of Len Affleck purchase of 12 Fountain Street, Cronulla. The costs component was $875.00 and the disbursements totalled $225.00. Total: $1100.00.

Office Account Cash Payments Book

Date of Payment	Cheque no.	Client name and matter description	Paid to	Purpose of payment	Ledger A/c no.	GST	Amount for ledger Taxable	Non-taxable	Total amount on face of cheque
20xx Jan 2	123456	Petty cash	Cash	Petty cash	PL6			200.00	200.00

Office Account Ledger

Account name: Petty cash
Account number: PL6

Date 20xx	Received from or paid to	Purpose	Ref. no.	DR	CR	DR/CR	Balance
Jan 2	Cheque cashed	Petty cash	P123456	200.00		DR	200.00

Petty cash Book Folio 1

Receipts 20xx	Date	Particulars	Ledger A/c no.	GST	Amount for ledger Taxable	Non-taxable	Total Payment
200.00	Jan 2	OFFICE – cash					
	2	Office refreshments Coffee and tea	PL8			8.60	8.60

Office Account Ledger

Account name: Office refreshments
Account number: PL8

Date 20xx	Received from or paid to	Purpose	Ref. no.	DR	CR	DR/ CR	Balance
Jan 2	Petty cash	Coffee and tea	PC1	8.60		DR	8.60

Costs Journal Folio 1

Date 20xx		Client	Particulars	Ledger A/c No.	Amount	
Feb	2	Len Affleck	Purchase 12 Fountain Street, Cronulla	CL1	875	00
Feb	5	Tommy Depp	Debt recovery Ichabod Krane	CL2	1,725	00

Post each entry to each client ledger account.

Office Account Ledger

Account name: Len Affleck
Purchase 12 Fountain Street, Cronulla
Account number: CL A1

Date 20xx	Received from or paid to	Purpose	Ref. no.	DR	CR	DR/ CR	Balance
Jan 25	To Speedy Enquiries	enquiries	PC123457	225.00		DR	225.00
Feb 2	Costs rendered		CJ1	875.00		DR	1,100.00

Account name: Tommy Depp
Debt recovery from Ichabod Krane
Account number: CL D1

Date 20xx	Received from or paid to	Purpose	Ref. no.	DR	CR	DR/ CR	Balance
Feb 5	Costs rendered		CJ1	1,725.00		DR	1,725.00

When each client pays the bill on 10 February, the amount paid will be entered via the office cash receipts book and then posted to the client ledger to give a nil balance.

Office Account Ledger

Account Name: Len Affleck
Purchase 12 Fountain Street, Cronulla
Account Number: CL A1

Date 20xx	Received from or paid to	Purpose	Ref. no.	DR	CR	DR/CR	Balance
Jan 25	To Speedy Enquiries	enquiries	P123457	225.00		DR	225.00
Feb 2	Costs rendered		CJ1	875.00		DR	1,100.00
Feb 10	By Affleck	Costs	R123492		1,100.00		Nil

Account name: Tommy Depp
Debt recovery from Ichabod Krane
Account number: CL D1

Date 20xx	Received from or paid to	Purpose	Ref. no.	DR	CR	DR/CR	Balance
Feb 5	Costs rendered		CJ1	1,725.00		DR	1,725.00
Feb 10	By Depp	Costs	R123493		1,725.00		Nil

At the end of the month, the costs recorded in the costs journal for that month are totalled and that total is posted in the private ledger account costs rendered as a credit. This entry will balance the sum of all the individual amounts that have been entered as debits in the individual clients' accounts.

2 On 5 February 20xx, you prepared a bill in accordance with your costs agreement in the debt recovery matter of Tommy Depp and Ichabod Krane. The costs component was $1,725.00. All disbursements were paid out of the trust account and so did not appear on the bill of costs.

Bill of costs

The LPA 2004 defines a bill of costs as a bill of costs for providing legal services. Costs include fees, charges, disbursements, expenses, and remuneration (s 302).

Any bill of costs prepared should be in accordance with the disclosure made by the solicitor and with any costs agreement made between the solicitor and client (see Chapter 2).

You can never have too much information in a bill of costs. A narrative at the beginning of a bill of costs will remind the client of all the good work you have completed for him or her.

Section 332 LPA provides that a bill may be in the form of a lump sum bill or an itemised bill. When a lump sum bill is prepared it describes the legal services completed by the law practice and specifies a total amount for those legal services. An itemised bill specifies in detail the legal services provided.

It is a requirement of s 332 that a bill must be signed on behalf of a legal practice by an Australian practitioner or an employee of the law practice. If the letter accompanying the bill has been signed then that is sufficient compliance with this section. Section 332(5) provides requirements for delivery of a bill.

To comply with s 333 LPA a bill must include or be accompanied by a written statement setting out the avenues which are open to the client in the event of a dispute in relation to legal costs. The statement must include details of costs assessment under Division 11, the setting aside of a costs agreement under s 328, and mediation under Division 8. It must also specify any time limits which apply to the taking of any action in a legal costs dispute. Of course each of these matters will have been disclosed under the disclosure of costs to clients required by s 309.

A law practice is permitted to charge interest on unpaid legal costs if the costs are unpaid at least 30 days after the practice has given a bill for the costs in accordance with Part 3.2 of the Act. Section 321(3) provides that interest may not be charged unless the bill for those costs contains the rate of interest and a statement that interest is payable. The maximum rate of interest which can be charged is 9% and is set out in cl 110A LPR.

Section 331 provides that a law practice must not commence legal proceedings to recover legal costs until at least 30 days after the law practice has given a bill which complies with s 332 and 333. The only exception to this is where the Court is satisfied a bill has been given and the person is about to leave this jurisdiction. Section 331 applies whether or not the costs are the subject of a costs agreement.

The effect of failing to disclose to a client anything required by Division 3 of Part 3.2 is that the client need not pay the legal costs until they have been assessed under Division 11. This would include the non-disclosure of the rate of interest charged on unpaid costs.

When preparing a bill you should include the following details:

(a) a description of the legal service provided;

(b) the total amount of the costs charged;

(c) any intended claim for interest if the costs are not paid, including the rate of interest (s 321 LPA);

(d) a statement setting out the following avenues open to the client in the event of a costs dispute

(i) that the client may apply to have the costs assessed under Division 11;

(ii) the setting aside of a costs agreement under s 328; and

(ii) mediation under Division 8 (s 331).

The statement must stipulate that an application for costs assessment must be made within 60 days after the bill was given, the request for payment was made, or the costs were paid in full (whichever is earliest) (s 350(4) and s 331(b))

Additional information which might be included is:

(d) the work done in providing the legal services;

(e) the period over which that work was done;

(f) the identity of the persons who did that work (including the position of the person, for example, partner or associate);

(g) the basis on which the costs have been calculated and charged (whether on a lump sum basis, an hourly basis, on items of work basis, a part of proceedings basis, or other basis);

(h) the facts relied on to justify the costs charged by reference to the above, the practitioner's skill, labour and responsibility, the complexity, novelty or difficulty of the matter, the quality of the work done, or any other relevant matter.

After a brief description of the work carried out, the basis on which the costs are calculated, a lump sum figure of the professional costs should be stated. Next, you should list under the heading 'disbursements' prepared from the client's office ledger account all disbursements which remain outstanding. In some matters, you may have a further heading 'future disbursements' or 'estimated disbursements', where you will list disbursements which will be incurred in the near future. Any disbursements that have been paid from the trust account should NOT appear on the memorandum of costs and disbursements. These disbursements will appear on the trust account statement required by cl 82 of the LPR. In many instances, you will need to prepare a trust statement at the same time as the bill of costs. A trust statement and a bill of costs may be prepared on the same page with one signature at the end. Note that there is no 'yours faithfully' on a bill of costs (or on a trust statement).

According to s 319(2) the law practice cannot charge for the preparation of bills of costs.

GST and the bill of costs

Another item which must appear on the bill is the GST payable on the total cost of the supply of legal services. This should cover professional costs and disbursements (where applicable). Practitioners will need to determine whether the disbursement is one which has been paid to a third party as agent for the client. If this is the case, then GST is not added. Other disbursements will need to have GST added.

Where the bill of costs is to serve as a tax invoice then it must be prepared in a way which satisfies the requirements of the legislation (please see A new Tax System Goods and Services Tax Regulations 1999). The following information must be included on the tax invoice, where the invoice is for more than $1000.00:

(a) the words 'tax invoice' stated prominently;
(b) the supplier's ABN;
(c) the date of issue of the tax invoice;
(d) the name of the supplier;
(e) the name of the recipient;
(f) the address or ABN of the recipient;
(g) a brief description of each thing supplied;
(h) the quantity of each thing supplied;
(i) the price of the supply.

In those firms where accounting for the GST is on a cash basis, no recording of GST is required at the time of sending the bill. This means that there is no recording of the GST component in the Costs Journal. When the bill is paid, the GST component will be recorded in the cash book and then in the GST ledger. Here is an example of a bill of costs and disbursements.

Bill of Costs

Potter and Associates

ABN 12345

'Tax Invoice'

2 February 20xx

Our Ref:
Your Ref:

Mr L Affleck
17 Mars Road
BUNDEENA NSW 2230

Your Purchase 12 Fountain Street, Cronulla

To our costs in this matter including receiving instructions, negotiating special conditions, exchanging contracts and settlement, in accordance with our costs agreement dated 4 January 20xx	875.00
GST	87.50
	962.50
Disbursements	
Speedy Enquiries	225.00
Balance due and owing	1,187.50

With compliments
Potter and Associates
Per: Signature of partner

Interest: If this bill is not paid within 30 days interest may be charged at the rate of 9 % prescribed by regulation 110A of the Legal Profession Regulation 2005.

In the event of a costs dispute the following avenues are open to you:

- costs assessment under Division 11 Legal Profession Act 2004;
- the setting aside of a costs agreement under s 328; and
- mediation under Division 8.

An application for costs assessment must be made within 60 days after the bill was given, the request for payment was made, or the costs were paid in full (whichever is earliest).

A transfer from trust to office

Sometimes when you send a bill of costs to a client, there will be money in that client's trust account for that matter. Whether you can use those trust funds to pay for professional costs is governed by s 261(1)(b) of the LPA and cl 88 of the LPR.

Section 261(1) provides:

> A law practice may do any of the following in relation to trust money held in a general trust account or controlled money account of the practice for a person:
>
> (b) withdraw money for payment to the practice's account for legal costs owing to the practice if the procedure prescribed in the regulations is complied with,
>
> ...

The prescribed procedure referred to is contained in cl 88 of the LPR.

Clause 88 provides that a law practice may withdraw the trust money if :

- the money is withdrawn in accordance with a costs agreement or instructions authorising the withdrawal; or
- the money is owed to the practice to reimburse it for money already paid by the practice; and
- before effecting the withdrawal the practice gives a request for payment, referring to the proposed withdrawal;
- the practice has given the person a bill relating to the money and no objection has been made within seven days;
- if a person does object within the seven days but has not applied for a review of the legal costs under the Act within 60 days;
- the money otherwise becomes legally payable.

If given in writing the instructions must be retained as a permanent record. If the instructions are not in writing then they must be reduced to writing no later than five days after the law practice effects the withdrawal. A copy must be retained as a permanent record.

When you prepare your bill you should show any credit balance in the client's trust ledger. You can refer to a proposed transfer of trust money so that the bill will show the actual amount owing.

Here is an example of a bill of costs where there is money in the client's trust account at the time of preparing the bill :

Bill of Costs

Potter and Associates

ABN 12345

'Tax Invoice'

2 February 20xx

Our Ref:
Your Ref:

Mr L Affleck
17 Mars Road
BUNDEENA NSW 2230

Your Purchase 12 Fountain Street, Cronulla

To our costs in this matter including receiving instructions, negotiating special conditions, exchanging contracts and settlement, in accordance with our costs agreement dated 4 January 20xx	875.00
GST @ 10%	87.50
	962.50

Disbursements

Speedy Enquiries	225.00
Total	1,187.50
Less amount to be transferred from trust on receipt of your authority	500.00
Balance due and owing	687.50

With compliments

Potter and Associates

Per: Signature of partner

After the expiration of seven days from the date of delivery of this bill we intend to withdraw the money held in trust for you and apply it towards payment of this bill unless you object to the bill.

Interest: If this bill is not paid within 30 days interest may be charged at the rate of 9% prescribed by regulation 110A of the Legal Profession Regulation 2005.

In the event of a costs dispute the following avenues are open to you:

- costs assessment under Division 11 Legal Profession Act 2004;
- the setting aside of a costs agreement under s 328; and
- mediation under Division 8.

An application for costs assessment must be made within 60 days after the bill was given, the request for payment was made, or the costs were paid in full (whichever is earliest).

When the terms of cl 88 have been complied with, the transfer procedure is:

1 (i) write a trust cheque and complete the butt (several transfers from several ledger accounts can be included in the one cheque, with each ledger account shown in the cash book; alternatively, several transfers can be made to a special trust ledger account by journal entry and, from there, by one cheque to office);
   (ii) record that cheque in the trust cash payments book as a payment;
   (iii) record the amount in the trust client's ledger account as a debit.

2 (i) write an office receipt for the cheque and write an office bank deposit slip including the cheque and bank the cheque;
   (ii) record the receipt details in the office cash receipts book as a receipt;
   (iii) record the amount of the receipt in the office client's ledger account as a credit.

Remember the trust account and the office account are entirely separate accounts.

Office ledger

The office ledger follows the same principles as the trust ledger. In the office system, it is convenient to divide the ledger into two parts:

1 the private ledger or business ledger (PL);

2 the client ledger (CL).

The private ledger is that part of the ledger which we use for any office expenses such as rent, stationery, capital contributions by the partners, or postage. These all relate to the carrying on of the business of being a legal practitioner.

The private ledger accounts will generally be a record of expenditure which will not be recovered. These ledger accounts will always be in debit.

In the private ledger, take care with the petty cash ledger and the costs rendered ledger. The only time postings will be made in the petty cash ledger will be when a cheque is drawn to put money into petty cash and when the total payments are recorded at the end of the month.

The costs rendered ledger is posted with the total costs for the month at the end of the month.

Each client matter will have a client ledger. On those occasions when a disbursement is incurred in a matter where there is insufficient money in trust, then that disbursement will be paid out of the office account. An entry will be made in the office cash payments book and then it will be posted as a debit to the client's ledger.

The client ledger accounts should eventually balance out to nil by the client paying the costs and disbursements.

When posting to the office account ledger, make sure you complete all the details in each column. The reference column is for the receipt number or cheque number. The column headed 'DR/CR' next to the 'balance' column, refers to the balance, not whether the posting is a debit or a credit.

Remember, in the office account, the only ledgers that will have a credit balance are the capital accounts of the partners and the costs rendered account. All other ledgers will be nil or in debit. If you find you have an office ledger in credit (apart from capital or costs rendered), you have made an error – probably, you have transferred too much money from trust to office. If so, you are in breach of the LPA, as money which was given to you, on trust, is now in your office account.

General journal

Practitioners use this journal to record financial entries of a non-cash nature. It is used for the same purpose as the trust journal to show the movement of money from one ledger account to another. At times, credit facilities may be used in the purchase of an asset or expense. To reflect a current financial position, the purchase must be recorded and this is where that occurs.

General Journal Folio GJ1

Date 20xx	Particulars	Folio	Debit	Credit
27 Jan	Office equipment Computer Works computers	PL9 PL10	6,300.00 6,300.00	

Office Account Ledger

Account name: Office Equipment
Account no: PL9

Date 20xx	Received from or paid to	Purpose	Ref. no.	DR	CR	DR/CR	Balance
27 Jan	Owed to Computer Works	Purchase computers	GJ1	6,300.00		DR	6,300.00

Account name: Computer Works
Account no: PL10

Date 20xx	Received from or paid to	Purpose	Ref. no.	DR	CR	DR/CR	Balance
27 Jan	Owed re purchase 3 Computers	Credit terms	GJ1		6,300.00	CR	6,300.00
28 Jan	to Computer Works	1st instalment on computers	P359276	630.00		CR	5,670.00

The journal is also used to correct errors in ledgers and is used in the preparation of financial accounts.

If a law firm contracted with Computer Works for the purchase of three computers which the firm had agreed to buy for $6,300 – payable by ten monthly instalments of $630, the detail would be recorded as follows:

These entries record in the ledger that you have acquired an asset (computers) valued at $6,300.00 as well as a liability to pay Computer Works $6,300.00 by instalments. The two ledger accounts must be set up. Remember that nothing can appear in the ledger without coming through a journal or cash book. At the time of acquiring the asset and incurring a liability, no cash payment has been made and no costs are involved. This leaves the general journal to record the transaction.

7 Balancing the Books

Reconciliation of trust records – cl 72

Trust records relating to the general trust account must be reconciled at the end of each month. Clause 72(3) states that the statements required by the regulation must be prepared within 15 working days after the end of the month. A law practice must retain the statements prepared. Apart from this legislative requirement, the balancing of the cash book is the first step to check the accuracy of the firm's accounting records.

There are a number of methods which can be used to produce a cash book balance. Two of those methods are discussed below.

(i) *Cash book summary*

To prepare a cash book summary you must:

1 total the receipts for the month;

2 record that total after the last entry for the month: date, total receipts;

3 total the payments for the month;

4 record that total after the last entry for the month: date, total payments;

5 prepare the cash book summary on the cash payments book after the Total Payments entry:

Cash Book Summary

Opening balance		$
Plus receipts for month of	____________	$
Less payments for month of	____________	$____________
Closing balance		$____________

The opening balance is the closing balance from the previous month. This will be found in the cash book control account ledger;

6 post the total receipts for the month to the cash book control account in the ledger. This will be posted in the DEBIT column;

7 post the total payments for the month to the cash book control account in the ledger. This will be posted in the CREDIT column;

8 record the closing balance in the BALANCE column.

(ii) *Cash book balance*

1 Total each of the final two columns of the cash receipts book. The 'amount' column will be the total receipts for that month only. The 'banking' column will be the total of the receipts for that month together

with the balance from the previous month. Record the date, total receipts, and the cash book control ledger account reference.

2 Total the final column of the cash payments book. Record the date, total payments, and the cash book control ledger account.
3 On the cash payments book, calculate the difference between the total of the receipts (using the figure in the bank column which includes the opening balance) and the total of the payments. This difference is the cash book balance.
4 Enter the cash book balance at the top of the cash receipts book for the next month. If the cash book is overdrawn, the balance is recorded as the first entry of the cash payments book.
5 Where a ledger account is being used to record monthly balances in the bank account, post to that ledger account. The total receipts are posted as a debit and the total payments are posted as a credit. Post the balance.

Either method of balancing the cash book can be used, both in the trust account and the office account. The cash book summary method is perhaps a more straightforward method of calculating the balance.

In the office account, the additional columns (GST, Taxable Amount for Ledger, Non-Taxable Amount for Ledger) need to be totalled and recorded on the cash book. The GST amounts on both receipts and payments sides must be totalled and posted to the GST ledger account.

Balancing the petty cash book

At the end of each month, the petty cash book must be balanced. The procedure is much the same as calculating the balance in the cash book.

Once again, it helps if you visualise the petty cash tin and the $200 we put in there:

1 total the payments which have been made during the month and record the figure in the petty cash book. This figure is posted to the petty cash ledger as a credit;
2 deduct the total payments from the total amount of cash which has been put into petty cash. This amount is referred to as the balance. If the petty cash tin was in front of you, it would be possible to count the money left. Record this amount (the 'balance') under the total payments for the month;
3 in the petty cash book, the total payments must be added to the balance, which will then equal the total receipts for the month. This is shown on the same line of the petty cash book;
4 the balance for the month must then be brought down in the left hand receipts column in readiness for the transactions in the next month;

5 the GST column must be totalled and posted to the GST ledger account as a debit.

See the setting out in the specimen accounts for Potter and Associates.

Balancing the costs journal

The end of month calculations for the costs journal are very straightforward.

Simply total the costs rendered for the month. Remember the costs journal is the record of all the bills you have sent out. It is irrelevant for the month end totals whether those costs have, in fact, been paid.

In the total in the costs journal, you do not include the total from the previous month.

When you have calculated the total for the month, this must be posted as a credit to the costs rendered ledger. This will balance the total of all those individual amounts which have been posted to the debit of the individual ledger accounts. The balance in the costs rendered ledger will keep a record of the total amount in costs you have billed during a certain period.

Bank reconciliation statement

Bank statements are prepared by the bank. The statement records for each particular account on each day, the total banked, and the cheques presented to the bank. The amounts that a law practice deposits with the bank will be recorded on the credit side of the practice's account. This recognises the bank's liability. Only the total of the deposit on any one day will be shown on the bank statement. That is, if, for example, three cheques are banked, only the total amount of those three cheques will appear in the credit column of the statement.

When a cheque drawn on a law practice's account is presented to the bank, reducing the liability of the bank, it will be recorded on the debit side of the solicitor's account.

The records maintained by a solicitor and the bank will have the same information however on different sides of the ledger. There may also be a time difference between entries in the law practice's books and entries in the bank's books. There will be a difference in time between a cheque being drawn and presented to the bank. Similarly, there may be a difference with the receipt of a deposit if the next banking is not until the following day. These differences create the basis for bank reconciliation statements. A bank reconciliation is prepared by comparing the law practice's records and the bank's records. It is a means of checking that the firm's accounting records agree with those records prepared by the bank.

Clause 72(2)(a) of the LPR requires a law practice at the end of each month to prepare a statement reconciling the balance of his or her trust bank account with the balance of the related cash book. The statement must be prepared within 15 working days of the end of the month and show the date of preparation.

To prepare a bank reconciliation:

1 check that all receipts and payments have been entered into the cash book;

2 prepare the cash book summary;

3 request bank statement for end of month;

4 compare the bank statement with the cash book:

   (i) tick entries which are common to the bank statement and cash book. Remember you will be comparing the credit side of the bank statement with the 'banked' column for the cash receipts book. You compare the debit side of the bank statement with the 'cheque amount' column for the cash payments book;

   (ii) list entries that appear in the bank statement which are not recorded in the cash book;

   (iii) list entries in cash book that do not appear in the bank statement. If these items are in the cash receipts book they are referred to as outstanding deposits. If these items are in the cash payments book, they are referred to as unpresented cheques;

5 complete the reconciliation statement. Set out below is a format that can be followed. It begins with the bank statement closing balance.

The Regulation does not state where you show the reconciliation. All accounting records should be kept together in a conveniently located place:

Potter and Associates
Bank reconciliation statement for the
period ended————————

	$	
Bank statement balance as at———/———/———		Cr
Add outstanding deposit(s)		
Add/less Item(s) in bank statement not in cash book Less unpresented cheque(s) (List separately showing date, cheque number, and amount)		
Add/less Item(s) in cash book not in bank statement		
Reconciled cash book balance	$————	
Date of Preparation	By	

The list of outstanding deposits must be made showing alongside each deposit the date in the cash book.

The list of unpresented cheques must include the cheque number together with the amount and the date drawn.

Generally, if the bank shows its balance as a credit on the statement, the solicitor's bank ledger account will show that balance as a debit. Clause 72(2)(b) of the LPR states that the reconciled cash book balance is required to be shown on the trial balance.

All practitioners should examine the bank reconciliation and the comparison at the end of the month to ensure that there are no anomalies. A law practice should ensure that arrangements have been made with the Bank (and followed) to charge the cost of maintaining the trust account to the office account.

Action should be taken by you if you find discrepancies between your records and those of the bank:

- any outstanding deposits should be banked on the next day;
- adjustments to be made by the bank for any incorrect charging of bank fees (items which are bank errors should not be recorded in the cash book and posted to a ledger account. They should be shown as an adjusting item in the bank reconciliation statement);
- any telegraphic transfer recorded in the bank statement and not in the cash book must be recorded on the next day in the cash book;
- any cheque that has not been presented for three months since the date of drawing should be followed up.

Bank charges

One of the items on the bank statement will be a debit for the fee the bank charges for keeping all current accounts. A law practice must instruct its bank to debit all bank fees for both the trust account and the office account from the office account. If bank fees were debited from the trust account then there would be a breach of the Act and Regulations. If the bank did charge bank fees or other charges to the trust account you would have to take immediate action and transfer money from office to trust to cover the debit.

As part of the end of month balancing procedures you must enter any bank fees shown on the Office Account Bank Statement, into the Office Account Cash Payments Book. The date of the entry will be the date on the bank notice and will usually be the last day of the month. Instead of a cheque number you will write 'Bank Notice' in the cheque number column. A ledger, 'Bank Fees and Charges', will have to be created in the Private Ledger of the Office Account and a posting made in the usual way.

Trial balance

Clause 72(2)(b) of the LPR requires a statement reconciling the balance of the trust ledger accounts with the balance of the practice's trust account cash books. This is referred to as a trial balance. The trial balance must be prepared monthly and within 15 working days of the end of the month.

A trial balance will show whether the system is in balance. It will detect errors (but by no means all possible errors) in the firm's internal records. One of the most common errors is where an entry has been posted to the wrong side of the ledger, that is, posted as a debit instead of a credit. In other instances, the problem may be in a transposition error, such as posting $25 as $52.

If a variance is found between the trial balance and the reconciled cash book balance, it could mean that insufficient funds are in the bank to meet commitments to clients. If there is an excess in the bank balance, it would mean that some transaction has not been recorded in the ledger.

A trial balance is a list of all accounts in the ledger with a balance other than nil. As each entry in the ledger is posted twice, once as a debit and once as a credit and the balance of each account is calculated from the debits and credits posted to that account, the total of all the debit balances should equal the total of all the credit balances.

To prepare a trial balance:

1 check all entries have been made in the cash book and posted to the appropriate ledger accounts;
2 prepare the cash book summary, including posting to the cash book control account (in the office account, you will need also to balance the petty cash book and the costs journal and post the balance to the appropriate ledger accounts);
3 check all journal entries have been posted to the ledger;
4 on a separate sheet of paper, with the headings as set out below, list the total of each individual ledger with a balance other than nil;
5 add each of the balances to find the total trial balance;
6 for the trust trial balance, compare the total of the trial balance with the cash book balance. They should be equal.

Clause 72(2)(b) stipulates the following information must be included in the trial balance:

- a list of the practice's trust ledger accounts showing the name, identifying reference and balance of each and a short description of the matter to which each relates;
- the date of preparation.

Here is a specimen trust trial balance.

Potter and Associates

Trust trial balance as at——————————

Matter no.	Account name	Matter description	Amount
A1	Appleby	Purchase 1 Fig Lane, Pyrmont	1,500.00
B1	Beasley	Discrimination	850.00
G2	Grozier	Shoplifting Charges	500.00
J1	Jones	Sale 3 Bell Close, Windsor	800.00
M4	Mitra	Property Settlement	550.00

Q1	Quirk	Third Party – G.I.O.	1,000.00
S5	Sun	Purchase business 'Con's Deli'	1,500.00
			6,700.00

Prepared by——————— Dated———————

Clause 72(2)(b) (i) Comparison

Total client ledger accounts	6,700.00
Reconciled cash book balance	6,700.00
Variance (should be nil)	NIL

Prepared by——————— on———————

Although it is not required by the Regulation, each partner should sign the trial balance. It does not make them liable for any error in the accounts for that follows as a matter of law. It is to record that each partner has checked the trial balance.

Some firms include the balance of the cash book control account in the trust trial balance. It will be a debit balance and should be the same figure as the total of all the other ledger accounts.

When preparing the trial balance in the office account, there will be two columns instead of the heading 'amount'. One column will be for all the debit balances (the majority of accounts in the office ledger) and one column will be for all the credit balances (these will be the capital account(s) and the cost rendered account):

Matter no.	Account name	Matter description	DR	CR

Note that in the office account, you do not prepare a comparison of the trial balance total with the cash book balance.

The balance of the cash book control account is included in the list of debit balances in the office trial balance.

An example of an office account trial balance is in the specimen accounts.

8 Controlled Money

Trust money deposited into a general trust account in New South Wales at an ADI will not earn any interest for the client. All interest on money in a general trust account at an ADI is payable to the Law Society on account of the Public Purpose Fund (s 288).

Some clients prefer that their money be deposited into an account that will earn them interest. In these cases, where the client directs the solicitor to deal with money in a particular way whereby the solicitor will continue to control that money, that money will be 'controlled money'.

Section 243(1) LPA defines controlled money as money received or held by a law practice in respect of which the law practice has a written direction to deposit the money in an account (other than a general trust account) over which the law practice has or will have exclusive control. It is in s 256 that we find that a law practice must deposit controlled money in the account specified in the written direction, as soon as possible after receiving it. The controlled money must be held exclusively for the person on whose behalf it was received. It must not be disbursed except in accordance with a written direction. The law practice must maintain the controlled money account and account for the controlled money as required by the regulations. In addition, the law practice must keep any written direction for the period prescribed by the regulation. Clause 77 stipulates that period to be seven years after finalisation of the matter to which it relates. If there is no written direction then the law practice should deposit the money into the general trust account.

Whereas the regulations allow the money in a general trust account to be deposited into the one account, a separate controlled money account must be opened with an ADI for each person who gives the law practice controlled money (s 256(6)).

Clauses 75 to 80 of the LPR 2005 set out the way in which a law practice must record the receipt and withdrawal of controlled money.

When establishing a controlled money account cl 75 specifies that the controlled money account must be maintained under an account name that includes the following particulars:

(a) the name of the law practice;

(b) the expression controlled money account;

(c) particulars sufficient to identify the purpose of the account and to distinguish the account from other accounts maintained by the law practice.

Any controlled money account opened before 1 October 2005 does not need to add the expression 'controlled money account' to the name of the account.

The sequence of records to be prepared can be shown as follows:

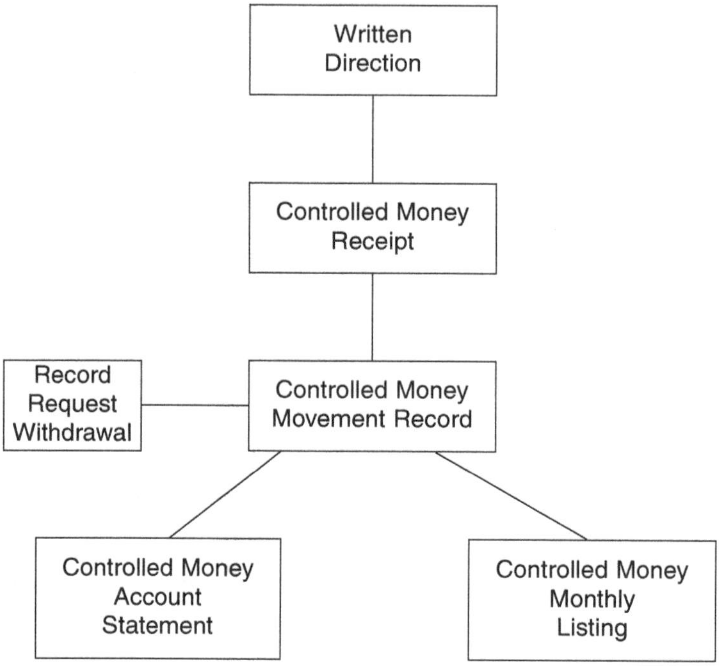

Controlled money receipt – cl 76

When a law practice receives controlled money it must issue a receipt as soon as possible. If money is paid into a controlled money account by direct deposit then the law practice must issue a receipt upon receipt of notice or confirmation of the deposit from the bank.

According to the regulation the law practice must operate a single controlled money receipt system for the receipt of all controlled money.

Subclause 6 sets out the particulars required for a controlled money receipt:

(a) the date of the receipt, and if different, the date of receipt of the money;

(b) the amount of money received;

(c) the form in which the money was received;

(d) the name of the person from whom the money was received;

(e) details clearly identifying the name of the person on whose behalf the money was received and the matter description and matter reference;

(f) particulars sufficient to identify the purpose for which the money was received;

(g) the name of and other details clearly identifying the controlled money account to be credited, unless the account has not been established by the time the receipt is made out;

(h) the name of the law practice, or the business name under which the law practice engages in legal practice , and the expression 'controlled money receipt';

(i) the name of the person who made out the receipt;

(j) the number of the receipt.

In those situations when the controlled money account is established after the receipt is issued then the details of the account must be added to the duplicate receipt.

Receipts must be consecutively numbered, issued in sequence and made out in duplicate. The original receipt must be delivered on request to the person from whom the controlled money was received. Any controlled money receipt cancelled or not delivered must be retained.

A receipt is not required to be made out for any interest earned on the controlled money account.

This controlled money receipt, if completed correctly will comply with the regulation.

Controlled Money Receipt
Potter and Associates

Receipt No.
Date:
Received from
The sum of ——————————dollars and ————cents
$ ———————— Cash/Cheque/Direct deposit
For and on behalf of ——————————————
Matter No.——————————————————
Matter Description:——————————————
Purpose ————————————————————
Name of controlled money account to be credited:

Account No.——————————

Received by:
Name:
Potter and Associates
Law Practice
Controlled Money Receipt

Withdrawal of controlled money – cl 78 and cl 79

A withdrawal from a controlled money account must be effected by, under the direction of or with the authority of a principal of a law practice. If the principal is not available then it must be made in accordance with cl 78(1)(b).

For each withdrawal the following particulars must be recorded:

(a) the date and number of the transaction;

(b) the amount withdrawn;

(c) in the case of an electronic funds transfer – the name and number of the account to which the amount was transferred and the relevant BSB number;

(d) the name of the payee or where the payee is an ADI, the name or BSB number of the ADI and the name of the person receiving the benefit of the payment;

(e) details clearly identifying the name of the person on whose behalf the payment was made and the matter reference;

(f) particulars sufficient to identify the purpose for which the payment was made;

(g) the person or persons effecting, directing or authorizing the withdrawal.

Particulars should be recorded for each withdrawal, in order and maintained separately for each controlled money account.

A withdrawal from a controlled money account can be effected either by cheque or electronic funds transfer. The withdrawal is to be made in accordance with the written direction applying to the money.

A law practice may withdraw money from a controlled money account to reimburse the practice's legal costs. The method that must be followed is set out in cl 88.

Controlled money register – cl 80

A law practice must maintain a controlled money register. This register is to record controlled money movements, notifications of interest and bank statements. A separate record of controlled money movements must be maintained for each controlled money account. This can be achieved in the form of a ledger.

A record of controlled money movements (the ledger) must record the following information:

(a) the name of the person on whose behalf the controlled money is held;

(b) the person's address;

(c) particulars to identify the matter;

(d) any changes to the recorded information.

In subclause 4 the following particulars must be recorded on the ledger:

(a) the date the controlled money was received;
(b) the number of the receipt;
(c) the date the money was deposited in the controlled money account;
(d) the name of and other details clearly identifying the controlled money account;
(e) the amount of controlled money deposited;
(f) details of the deposit sufficient to identify the depositor;
(g) interest received;
(h) details of any payments from the controlled money account, including the particulars required to be recorded under clause 78(2).

If the following controlled money movement record is completed correctly, it will meet the particulars required by cl 80 of the LPR.

Controlled money movement record
Potter and Associates

Name ———————————— Matter no. ————————

Address————————————————————

Matter Description———————————————

Financial Institution———————————————

Address————————————————————

Original investment amount $—————— Date——/——/——

Account name——————————————————

Account no.——————————

Term/duration——————————

INTEREST: Rate——————————

Payable from——————————

Payable on——————————

Date Rct Rec'd/ Paid	Form & Ref.	Receipt Number	Pd to/ Received from/ Purpose	Authority	Debit W/d	Credit Dep.	Balance

Controlled money listing – cl 80(8)

A law practice must, within 15 working days after the end of each month, prepare and keep as a permanent record a statement containing a list of the practice's controlled money accounts detailing:

- the name, number, and balance of each account in the register; and
- the name of the person on whose behalf the controlled money in each account was held; and
- a short description of the matter to which each account relates.

The statement must show the date it was prepared.

Controlled money account statement – cl 82

A law practice must furnish a controlled money account statement to each person on whose behalf controlled money is held. This requirement is identical to the requirement to provide a trust account statement for accounts in the general trust account and is discussed in Chapter 3.

9 Legal Profession Act 2004

Unclaimed trust funds – s 266

A law practice should review a client's trust records at the completion of each matter. All balances should be nil and there should be no unpresented cheques relating to the matter on either the trust or office account bank reconciliation. This will assist in reducing the amount of unclaimed trust money which a practice must deal with.

From time to time, a practitioner will discover money in the trust account which is considered to be unclaimed funds.

Section 266 of the LPA provides:

1 If a law practice holding money in a trust account cannot find the person on whose behalf the money is held or a person authorised to receive it, the practice may:
   (a) pay the money to the Treasurer for credit to the Consolidated Fund; and
   (b) provide the Treasurer with such information as the Treasurer requires in relation to the money and the person on whose behalf the money is held by the practice.
2 If the law practice pays the money to the Treasurer under subsection (1) the practice is relieved from any further liability in relation to the money;
3 The Treasurer must pay money deposited under this section to a person who satisfies the Treasurer as to his or her entitlement to the money;

Note that there is no obligation on the solicitor to pay the money to the Treasurer; this section only states that the solicitor 'may' pay the money to the Treasurer.

Public purpose fund – s 284

Every law practice in New South Wales which operates a trust account must comply with s 283 of the LPA and deposit with the Law Society an amount calculated in accordance with clauses 96 to 101 of the LPR. Briefly, this amount is calculated with reference to the lowest balance recorded in the trust account kept by the firm during the previous 12 months ending on 31 March and the amount (if any) on deposit by the practice with the Society on the day on which the lowest balance is recorded.

Section 284 provides that the Law Society may invest this money and the interest is to be paid into the 'Public Purpose Fund' (s 284(4)).

Section 289 deals with payments from the Fund. Payments of certain costs and expenses which may be made from the Fund are listed in s 290. It is in s 292 that the discretionary payments which may be made from the Fund are found. These include payments to the Legal Aid Fund, the Fidelity Fund, the Law Foundation Fund, the promotion and furtherance of Legal Education in New South Wales and the furtherance of law reform.

Legal Profession Regulation 2005

External Examiner's Report (Division 7)

Clauses 92 to 95 deal with the requirements for an External Examiner's Report on Trust Money. A Report is required where the law practice has received, disbursed, or held trust money during the 12 month period to March 31 and must be lodged with the legal practitioner's application for renewal of practising certificate. A final examination must be made when the law practice ceases to be authorized to receive trust money or ceases to engage in legal practice in New South Wales.

At the time of making the report, the examiner must complete an extensive checklist to be retained with the accounting records of the solicitor. The checklist is to test the compliance of the accounts with the LPR.

If a law practice has received or held transit money only, then it is not required to lodge an External Examiner's Report.

10 Other Records

Section 703 of the LPA 2004 provides for the Law Society Council to make rules with respect to the engaging in legal practice as a solicitor. The rules are the Revised Professional Conduct and Practice Rules and failure to comply with them may lead to a finding of professional misconduct or unsatisfactory profession conduct. The rules may be accessed via the Law Society of New South Wales home page.

The LPR 2005 and the Revised Professional Conduct and Practice Rules 1995 set out information which must be contained in the accounting and other records maintained by legal practitioners. These rules apply whether or not trust money as defined in s 243 LPA has been received.

File register – r 13

As soon as practicable after receiving instructions, a practitioner is required to open a file for documentation and provide in the file the following information:

- full name and address of the person;
- date of receipt of instructions;
- a brief description of the services to be provided; and
- an identifier.

The name and address of the person are to be entered in a file register together with the identifier. The identifier should preferably be a number and it should be prefixed with the last two digits of the year in which the instructions are received. This will assist recovery of files.

A file register provides a history in relation to all matters conducted by a firm.

Safe custody register – r 14

When a practitioner is handed possession of an important document such as a deed or will, or some other valuable property, to be held in safe custody, the practitioner must maintain a safe custody register. The register must contain the following:

- name and address of person;
- a short description of the item held;
- date on which item received by practitioner;
- the number of the safe custody packet in which the item is held.

Although it is not a requirement, it is important to record the date on which the document was handed up.

Register of financial interests – r 15

At the principal place of practice a register must be maintained which must disclose the name and other identifying particulars of any company, partnership, or other entity in which the practitioner has a financial interest and which engages in any dealing with trust money or controlled money received by the practitioner or the firm.

Inspection of registers – r 16

It is by virtue of r 16 that a Trust Account Inspector or an investigator appointed in accordance with Part 3 Division 3 of the LPA can request a law practice to produce for inspection any file register, safe custody register, or financial register maintained by the practice.

The registers required by the Rules may be maintained in electronic form, provided that they can be produced in visible form on demand. Visible form here means production of information in permanent legible form in the English language.

Other registers

Although not required by any rule, there are a number of other registers which are useful to maintain. Costs for items such as photocopying, facsimiles and STD/IDD telephone calls must be collected for inclusion in the bill of costs issued to the client and a convenient way to do this is to keep a register.

11 Goods and Services Tax ('GST')

Legislation for the introduction of a Goods and Services Tax (GST) was passed into law on 8 July 1999. GST is governed principally by the A New Tax System (Goods and Services Tax) Act 1999. The GST applies at the rate of 10% on the supply of most goods and services consumed in Australia after 1 July 2000.

An entity carrying on a business is required to register for GST if its annual turnover is more than $50,000.00. The majority of legal work is a taxable supply. All practitioners need to ensure that they will be entitled to full recovery of GST. The full GST can be recovered if the costs agreement provides for this. Full recovery of GST requires the GST exclusive value of the supply to be identified and increased by 10%.

The performance of the majority of legal work is a taxable supply. As a consequence, GST is payable for legal work completed on or after 1 July 2000.

A costs agreement may provide that the rate or lump sum amount includes GST. If a rate or lump sum is GST exclusive, then each practitioner will need to make a specific provision for recovery of the GST in the costs agreement.

Disbursements will have to be categorized. Where disbursements are incurred by the solicitor in the course of making a supply of legal services to clients then those disbursements should be included in the value of the supply when GST is calculated.

Where amounts are paid to third parties with the solicitor acting as an agent, then, in this case, those amounts should be excluded from the figure on which GST for the legal services is calculated.

GST and the trust account

To determine the impact of GST on a legal practitioner's trust account, it will be necessary to identify who the contracting party is and the reason the money is being held. If the client is the contracting party, then the payment from the trust account is made as an agent. Here, the practitioner does not have to account for the GST. It is recommended that the solicitor has a retainer agreement with the client which addresses the issue of the solicitor acting as agent for the client.

Where, however, the contracting party is the practitioner, then the payment is made for a service provided by the practitioner and the payment from the trust account may satisfy a debt to the solicitor. In these circumstances, it is the responsibility of the solicitor to pass on GST to the client, as the practitioner is not the recipient of the supply and is not the contracting party. It is suggested that a practitioner should pay all money for which the practitioner is liable from the office account and then recover the full amount from the trust account. The transfer from trust should only be carried out after the payment has been made by the practitioner. If this method is followed, then there is no need for the trust account to account for the GST.

12 Practice Transactions

The best way to learn how to maintain trust and office accounts is to practice making the required entries and postings.

Set out below are a number of transactions of a fictional firm 'Potter and Associates'. To begin with, it would be a good idea for you to trace the entries and postings through the specimen accounts. The transactions can be used later to revise your knowledge of trust, controlled money and office book-keeping.

In January 20xx, Harriet Potter set up her own practice, having spent five years as an employed solicitor and then three years as a partner of a medium sized firm. She carried out the following transactions:

Transaction

10.01.xx to commence the office account, Harriet obtained a bank cheque (National Australia Bank, Sydney) for $30,000 as the capital of the firm and opened an office account with the UTS Bank. She asked for urgent clearance of the cheque (capital paid in is a liability of the firm, since capital money is owed to that partner. It is posted as a credit to the partner's ledger account);

10.01.xx Harriet prepared and banked office money received to-date;

14.01.xx Harriet paid Telstra $950 for the installation of telephones (as telephone installation is an expense of the firm, this is posted as a debit to the ledger account). The GST component of $95 will be recorded in the cash book and then posted to the GST ledger account at the end of the month;

14.01.xx as the first step towards furnishing the office, she bought from 'Mini Cost Officeworks Pty Ltd' some equipment, furniture, and other office items:

- two iMac computers for $1,995 each;
- one laser printer for $395;
- two desks for $950 each;
- one filing cabinet for $173;
- one bookcase for $565;
- ten packets of white paper totalling $40.

(Apart from stationery, these are items of a capital nature. Being assets, they are posted to the debit of the ledger accounts. Because different rates of depreciation for taxation purposes may apply, different ledger accounts will be used for office machines and furniture. The paper will have a different ledger too (office stationery));

14.01.xx Harriet cashed a cheque for $200 for petty cash (this cheque will not be crossed 'not negotiable', as Harriet needs cash in return. This is 'cash in hand' and is an asset. It is posted as a debit in the petty cash ledger).

(Note: in the specimen accounts, no specimen office cheques have been provided after this cheque.);

14.01.xx Harriet used some of the petty cash to purchase ground coffee and herbal tea. The total was $13.75;

14.01.xx the first money to be placed into Harriet Potter's trust account was received from Grollow Pty Ltd (registered office at 52 Park Street, Sydney). Daniel Grollow gave Harriet a company cheque for $13,000 drawn on the account of Grollow Pty Ltd with Commonwealth Bank, Haymarket, for costs and disbursements for the matter Grollow Pty Ltd Subdivision at Moore Park;

14.01.xx received from Ms Twyla Harp (2/21 Macleay Street, Potts Point) her personal cheque (St George Bank, Kings Cross), $2,500 for costs and disbursements in her matter of the incorporation of Twyla Harp Consultants Pty Ltd, a casting company;

14.01.xx received from Nat Damon (3 Australia Street, Camperdown), $825 in cash on account of costs. (The cash consisted of 8 × $100 and 1 × $20 +1 × $5.) Nat has been charged with offensive behaviour in a public place and has instructed Harriet to present a plea in mitigation at the end of the month;

prepared and banked trust money received to-date;

15.01.xx James and Jane Barnes are listing their five bedroom country-style residence at 5 Linlithgow Road, Point Piper. Harriet is instructed to draw up a contract for the sale by auction. She is also to act for James and Jane on the purchase of the penthouse at Rockwall Gardens, Potts Point. The purchase price at Rockwall Gardens is $1.7 million and the vendor is Rockwall Gardens Pty Ltd;

James and Jane give Harriet their personal cheque (St. George Bank, Bowral) for $175,000 being:

- $1,000 on account of costs and disbursements on the sale;
- $174,000 on account of the balance of deposit and costs and disbursements on the purchase;

15.01.xx Ms Trina Arena (71 Sutherland Road, Paddington) has instructed Harriet to act for her in a Family Court property matter. The travel which has been necessary for her career has been responsible for the breakdown of her marriage. Her husband is Marco Mendes. Harriet predicted that this will be a long, drawn-out matter. Trina brings Harriet a bank cheque for

$8,000 (Citibank, Oxford Street, Paddington) on account of costs and disbursements;

15.01.xx Mr Tim Hanks gave Harriet $9,500 cash to cover future disbursements in his personal injury matter. Tim lives at 15 Hollywood Drive, Birchgrove. Tim gives a written direction to deposit the money at call with Westpac Bank at an interest rate as determined by Westpac. At lunchtime, Harriet deposited the money with Westpac (Haymarket branch, 359 George Street), account number DO11395 at 8.2% fixed interest rate at call. Interest is to be credited monthly to the account (controlled money received in the form of cash is deposited directly to a controlled money account);

15.01.xx Nannette Benning (2 Norma Crescent, Maroubra) came to see Harriet. Her mother, Angela Ash, died last week. Nannette has been appointed her executor and doesn't know what should happen next. Nannette brought with her the will, an assortment of bills and the $5,460 cash she found in the tea caddy. Harriet wrote out a trust receipt. There were 50 × $100, 8 × $50 and 6 × $10;

15.01.xx a depressed Beryl Streep (5 Mason Avenue, Beecroft) has made an appointment to see Harriet. Last year, she had an operation performed on her right eye by Doctors A Smith and B Jones. The eye is, according to Beryl, 'wonderful, but my hand is a mess'. Due to the pain and lack of movement in the hand, Beryl has been unable to work since the operation. She needs Harriet's help. Beryl hands over $1,000 (her personal cheque, Commonwealth Bank, Beecroft) on account of costs and disbursements in a possible medical negligence case;

15.01.xx received by way of a telegraphic transfer from the Melbourne branch of Westpac Bank, $31,500, being the 10% deposit in Gwen Paltrow's sale of 6 Pacific Parade, Palm Beach, to Leonard Caprio. The deposit is being held in the Potter and Associates Law Practice trust account. There is no agent in the matter (as this is a direct deposit, there is no need to include a deposit slip).

(Note: in the specimen accounts, no specimen trust receipts have been provided after this receipt.);

15.01.xx Harriet prepared and banked trust money received to-date.

(Note: in the specimen accounts, no specimen trust bank deposit slips have been provided after this bank deposit slip.);

19.01.xx Nannette Benning was waiting for Harriet when she arrived at the office. Angela Ash had sold her car in the week before she died. Nannette wanted to give Harriet the cheque from the buyer, Jack Brabham. The cheque is for $12,500 (National Australia Bank, Coogee);

19.01.xx Harriet drew a trust cheque for $35 in favour of ASIC for reservation of name for Twyla Harp's matter;

19.01.xx	An account has been received from Quality Surveyors for survey fees in the Grollow Subdivision matter. Harriet draws a trust cheque for $3,575;
19.01.xx	Harriet applies for a s 149(2) certificate from Woollahra Council and draws a trust cheque for $40. She also draws a cheque for $20 to Sydney Water for a drainage diagram. These inquiries are for the contract in the Barnes sale. (Note: in the specimen accounts, no specimen trust cheques have been provided after this cheque.);
19.01.xx	at lunchtime, Harriet joined the queue at the Post Office and bought ten books of 45c stamps ($4.50 per book). She used money out of petty cash;
19.01.xx	in the afternoon, the adventurer Edward Hilary came into Harriet's office. Edward was anxious to have a will prepared straightaway, as he was leaving that night on his next mountain climbing adventure. Fortunately, Harriet was able to prepare the will immediately. Harriet handed Edward her bill for the preparation of the will together with the original executed will. In return, Edward gave her his personal cheque (Westpac Bank, Glebe) for $165 (including GST) (this money can go straight into Harriet's office account, as she has completed the work and prepared and delivered her bill to the client). (Note: in the specimen accounts, no specimen office receipts or office deposit slips have been provided after this receipt and deposit slip.);
19.01.xx	Harriet made a special trip to Rumpole Law Stationer's and purchased various bundles of legal forms. The cost of all the forms was $75.95. She paid $83.55 (including GST) out of petty cash;
19.01.xx	Noni Collette (2 Diver Crescent, Porpoise Heads) consulted Harriet in relation to a possible discrimination case against her employer, Fantasy Productions Pty Ltd. Harriet took instructions from her and requested $2,000 on account of costs and disbursements. Noni handed Harriet her personal cheque for $2,000 drawn on the National Australia Bank, Kings Cross;
19.01.xx	Harriet prepared a commercial lease for her client, Humungous Properties Pty Ltd (19 Bridge Street, Sydney). The tenant is to be Fidel Vista. Harriet prepared her bill of costs which totalled $1,335. The costs component was $423 (the only book-keeping entry to be made is for rendering the bill of costs);
19.01.xx	Harriet prepared and banked trust money received to-date;
20.01.xx	Sumi Jo (15 Sublime Street, Leura) was outraged by the way the Summer Bay Opera Theatre management treated her during her recent tour. Sumi Jo wants Harriet to 'sue their socks off. How dare they treat me like that'. Harriet advised her that she will have to look into the terms of the contract and get

further instructions. Sumi Jo hands Harriet a cheque for $2,750 on account of costs and disbursements;

20.01.xx times have been tough for Harriet's old friend Russell Rowe (1 Juno Parade, Alexandria). Russell has not had any work and has been unable to make any purchases. Russell had an audition coming up and the temptation was too great as he walked through the men's department of David Jones store. Russell was caught shoplifting. Harriet won't be charging anything for her time, but asked Russell for $440 which she knows will be counsel's fee on brief. Russell drew a personal cheque for $440;

20.01.xx Harriet received a contract from the vendor's solicitors for the sale of 85 Watkin Street, Newtown North. The vendor is Maggie Dench. Harriet's clients, Tom and Nicole Cridman (1 Yarra Avenue, Darling Point), are purchasing the property for $425,000.00. Harriet telephoned the Cridmans to come to the office to go through the contract. They gave Harriet their personal cheque for $43,500 to cover the deposit, costs and disbursements. Tom and Nicole instructed Harriet to deposit the cheque into her trust account until such time as it is required;

20.01.xx Harriet prepared and banked trust money received to-date;

22.01.xx as there was not much time before the exchange of contracts in the Cridman purchase, Harriet paid, by office account cheques, $125 to Speedy Enquiry Service for searches and $200 to Bug-a-lugs Pest Service for a pest report;

22.01.xx Harriet was instructed by Solita Davidovich, 12 Bright Street, Rozelle. Solita is the executrix of the will of her late mother, Tamara Davidovich. Probate has been granted. Tamara Davidovich held several bank accounts with the Commonwealth Bank. Solita brought with her a bank cheque for the total of these, $173,249.57. Solita instructs Harriet to invest this money with the National Australia Bank of Australia (357 George Street, Haymarket) at call until such time as all the other assets have been realised and an interim distribution can be made to the beneficiaries. Harriet carries out the instructions after receiving a written direction. The account is number 349–341–790. The interest rate is 8.5%;

24.01.xx Kelvin Spacey (2 Lois Lane, Parramatta) had earlier consulted Harriet in relation to a personal injury claim against Alberto Almodovar. Kelvin has now decided definitely to proceed with the matter and hands over a cheque for $10,000 to be put into trust. As time is about to expire, Harriet went to the District Court to file a statement of claim, paying the $377.00 filing fee from the office account;

24.01.xx Harriet drew an office account cheque in favour of Domain Realty, as managing agent for the office building. The cheque was for $1,925 for one month's rent ($1,750) plus GST;

24.01.xx	received a bank cheque from Alphonse Schwarz for $5,572 in settlement of a personal injury matter with client Drewe De Vito (15 Bower Street, Bankstown);
24.01.xx	a debt collected from Ivan Owen was paid by cheque to the firm for client Jonathon Malkovich (25 Georges Road, Hurstville). The bank cheque was for $15,750.00;
24.01.xx	Harriet completed a trust receipt for Yimou Zhang (17 Thomas Street, Haymarket) who is purchasing a business 'Flights of Fantasy' from Stephanie Spielberg. Yimou Zhang gave Harriet a personal cheque for $23,000, which will cover the deposit and the costs and disbursements of the matter;
25.01.xx	Harriet prepared and banked trust money received to date;
25.01.xx	Harriet paid $365 from the trust account to Seek and Search Pty Ltd for searches in a number of matters: • $50 for title searches in the Barnes sale at Point Piper; • $275 for searches in the Arena Family Court matter; • $40 for searches in the Ash Estate.
25.01.xx	Steve Boccho of counsel has requested that Harriet pay his fee for advice in the Collette discrimination matter. She draws a trust cheque for $550.00 in his favour;
26.01.xx	after receiving satisfactory searches and pest report (the Cridmans had specifically instructed not to get a building report), Harriet exchanged contracts on the Cridman purchase at Newtown. She drew a trust cheque for $42,000 (for the balance 10% deposit) in favour of Starr Realty Pty Ltd;
26.01.xx	Harriet received $1,335.00 from Fidel Vista to pay for stamp duty and registration of the lease and her costs of acting for Humungous Properties Pty Ltd. Humungous Properties Pty Ltd is Harriet's client and has substantial property holdings. Fidel Vista is leasing one of those properties, at Unit 1/7 Cook Way, Botany;
26.01.xx	Harriet prepared and banked trust money received to-date;
27.01.xx	Harriet paid by trust cheque $690.00 to ASIC for the incorporation fee in Twyla Harp Incorporation matter;
28.01.xx	Harriet went to the Office of State Revenue to stamp the lease in the Humungous Properties Pty Ltd and Vista matter. Stamp duty was assessed at $855.00, which was paid with a trust cheque;
28.01.xx	on the same day, Harriet went to the Department of Lands to register the lease in Humungous Properties Pty Ltd and Vista. Harriet drew a trust cheque for $57.00;
28.01.xx	Harriet's bank, UTS Bank, advised her that the cheque received from Russell Rowe on 20 January was not met on presentation and has been dishonoured. Harriet reverses the trust receipt;

28.01.xx Drewe De Vito came to Harriet's office. He was anxious to pick up a cheque in relation to the settlement of his personal injury matter against Alphonse Schwarz. Harriet gave him her bill of costs, showing $725.00 owing in costs (plus $72.50 GST). Drewe authorised Harriet to deduct her costs from the money held in trust. Harriet drew a trust cheque in De Vito's favour for the balance of $4,775.00;

28.01.xx Nat Damon's offensive behaviour charge was listed at Waverley Local Court. Harriet presented the plea in mitigation on his behalf. The magistrate imposed a fine in spite of Harriet's wonderful advocacy. Harriet gave Nat her bill of costs – $750.00 was noted as costs (plus $75.00 GST). Nat authorised Harriet to transfer costs owing from trust to office;

Harriet drew one trust cheque for $1,622.50 in favour of her office account, covering her costs plus GST in the De Vito matter and in the Damon matter;

28.01.xx the cupboard at home is getting very bare. Harriet draws an office account cheque for $550 for her drawings;

28.01.xx Harriet prepared and banked office money received to-date;

29.01.xx the Paltrow sale to Caprio matter was settled. The 10% deposit had been held by Harriet Potter as stakeholder. Gwen Paltrow is now entitled to that money. Gwen has decided to purchase a property at 2 Jonah Street, Whale Beach from the Renoufs. Gwen directs Harriet to transfer $30,000 from her trust ledger to the new matter Paltrow purchase 2 Jonah Street, Whale Beach to cover deposit, costs, and disbursements. Gwen is currently staying at her sister's place at 7 Riverview Road, Clareville.

(This is a trust account transfer journal entry. No money comes into or leaves the trust account. It is an internal transfer.);

30.01.xx the Cridmans gave instructions to prepare a draft contract to sell their current home and to transfer $1,000 from their purchase matter C2 to a new account relating to their sale. This is to cover part costs and disbursements in the sale matter; Nicole Cridman gave Harriet a bank cheque in favour of the Office of State Revenue for payment of stamp duty on their purchase. Nicole instructed Harriet that the contract should be stamped before 5 February. (The bank cheque in favour of the Office of State Revenue is transit money. A record of this transit money, including brief particulars sufficient to identify the transaction and its purpose needs to be made in the file. No extra accounting record required. If it is not paid to the Office of State Revenue before 5 February then the prescribed period will have lapsed. New instructions would then have to be received or the cheque banked into the general trust account. Harriet pays over the cheque within the prescribed time).

31.01.xx	Received a cheque for $15,000 from AMP Insurance Ltd for proceeds of life insurance policy on the late Angela Ash;
31.01.xx	Gwen Paltrow is going overseas for work and is not sure when she will return. She gives Harriet her sole power of attorney dated 31.01.xx. This includes the power to operate her personal bank account until her return.The account number is 123–456 and is with the Commonwealth Bank, Martin Place, Sydney. (An entry will need to be made in the Powers and Estates Register.);
31.01.xx	Cheque number 555609 Office Account cancelled prior to issue;
01.02.xx	Harriet prepared and banked trust money received 31 January 20xx;
01.02.xx	Harriet prepared a cash book summary for the trust account and the office account;
01.02.xx	Mrs Nannette Benning requested a trust statement of account as at this date;
03.02.xx	UTS Banking Corporation sent the bank statements for the trust account and the office account. Harriet prepared a bank reconciliation statement for the trust account and the office account;
03.02.xx	Harriet prepared a trial balance for the trust account and for the office account;
03.02.xx	Harriet prepared a controlled money listing of accounts.

Chapter 13

SPECIMEN ACCOUNTS FOR POTTER & ASSOCIATES

Potter and Associates Client Register			
Client name	**Address**	**Will held**	**Security documents packet**
Arena, Trina	71 Sutherland Road, Paddington	Y	N
Barnes, James & Jane	5 Linlithgow Road, Point Piper	Y Y	x6031 x6032
Benning, Nannette	2 Norma Crescent, Maroubra	N	N
Collette, Noni	2 Diver Crescent, Porpoise Heads	N	N
Cridman, Tom & Nicole	1 Yarra Avenue, Darling Point	Y Y	x6033 x6034
Damon, Nat	3 Australia Street, Camperdown	N	N
Davidorich, Solita	12 Bright Street Rozelle	N	N
De Vito, Drewe	15 Bower Street, Bankstown	Y	x6035
Grollow Pty Ltd	52 Park Street, Sydney	N	N
Harp, Twyla	2/21 Macleay Street, Potts Point	Y	x6036
Hilary, Edward	C/- PO Box 27, Glebe	Y	x6037
Hanks, Tim	15 Hollywood Drive, Birchgrove	N	N
Humungous Properties Pty Ltd	19 Bridge Street, Sydney	N	N
Jo, Sumi	15 Sublime Street, Leura	Y	x6038
Malkovich, Jonathon	25 Georges Road, Hurstville	N	N
Paltrow, Gwen	6 Pacific Beach, Palm Beach	Y	x6040
Rowe, Russell	1 Juno Parade, Alexandria	N	N
Streep, Beryl	5 Mason Avenue, Beecroft	N	N
Spacey, Kelvin	2 Lois Lane, Parramatta	N	N
Zhang, Yimou	17 Thomas Street, Haymarket	Y	x6039

Potter and Associates
Matter Register

	Matter no	Client name	Matter description	File ref	Date opened	Trust ref	Office ref	Date closed
A Category	A1	Arena, T	Family court property	xx/A1	15/01/xx	A1	xx/CL A1	
	A2	Benning, N executor Estate late Angela Ash	Estate late Angela Ash	xx/A2	15/01/xx	A2	xx/CL A2	
B Category	B1	Barnes, J & J	Purchase Potts Point	xx/B1	15/01/xx	B1	xx/CL B1	
	B2	Barnes, J & J	Sale Point Piper	xx/B2	15/01/xx	B2	xx/CL B2	
C Category	C1	Collette, N	Discrimination	xx/C1	19/01/xx	C1	xx/CL C1	
	C2	Cridman, T & N	Purchase Newtown	xx/C2	20/01/xx	C2	xx/CL C2	
	C3	Cridman, T & N	Sale Darling Point	xx/C3	30/01/xx	C3	xx/CL C3	

	Matter no	Client name	Matter description	File ref	Date opened	Trust ref	Office ref	Date closed
D Category	D1	Damon, N	Plea in mitigation	xx/D1	15/01/xx	D1	xx/CL D1	
	D2	Davidovich, S	Estate late Tamara Davidovich	xx/D2	22/01/xx		xx/CL D2	
	D3	De Vito, D	Personal injury	xx/D3	24/01/xx	D3	xx/CL D2	
G Category	G1	Grollow Pty Ltd	Subdivision at Moore Park	xx/G1	14/01/xx	G1	xx/CL G1	
H Category	H1	Harp, TM	Incorporation Twyla Harp Consultants	xx/H1	14/01/xx	H1	xx/CL H1	
	H2	Hilary, E	Will	xx/H2	19/01/xx		xx/CL H2	19/01/01
	H3	Hanks, TML	Personal injury litigation	xx/H3	15/01/xx		xx/CL H3	
	H4	Humungous Properties Pty Ltd	Commercial lease	xx/H4	26/01/xx	H4	xx/CL H4	
J Category	J1	Jo, S	Breach of contract	xx/J1	20/01/xx	J1	xx/CL J1	

	Matter no	Client name	Matter description	File ref	Date opened	Trust ref	Office ref	Date closed
M Category	M1	Malkovich, J	Debt collection	xx/M1	24/01/xx	M1	xx/CL M1	
P Category	P1	Paltrow, G	Sale Pacific Parade, Palm Beach	xx/P1	15/01/xx	P1	xx/CL P1	
	P2	Paltrow, G	Purchase Jonah St, Whale Beach	xx/P2	29/01/xx	P2	xx/CL P2	
	P3	Paltrow, G	Power of Attorney	xx/P3	31/01/xx			
R Category	R1	Rowe, R	Shoplifting charges	xx/R1	20/01/xx	R1	xx/CL R1	
S Category	S1	Streep, B	Medical negligence	xx/S1	15/01/xx	S1	xx/CL S1	
	S2	Spacey, K	Personal injury	xx/S2	24/01/xx	S2	xx/CL S2	
Z Category	Z1	Zhang, Y	Purchase business 'Fights of Fantasy'	xx/Z1	24/01/xx	Z1	xx/CL Z1	

Potter and Associates

Receipt: **71821**

Date: 14/01/20xx

TRUST ACCOUNT RECEIPT

Received from Grollow Pty Ltd

On 14/01/xx

the sum of Thirteen thousand dollars

$13,000.00 Cheque/~~Cash/Direct Deposit~~

For and on behalf of:

G1 : Grollow Pty Ltd : Subdivision at Moore Park

Matter no Account name Matter description

Reason: On account of costs and disbursements

Received by: H. Potter

On behalf of: Potter and Associates

Law Practice

Trust Account

Potter and Associates

Receipt: **71822**

Date: 14/01/20xx

TRUST ACCOUNT RECEIPT

Received from Ms Twyla Harp

On 14/01/xx

the sum of Two thousand five hundred dollars

$2,500.00 Cheque/~~Cash/Direct Deposit~~

For and on behalf of:

H1 : Harp : Incorporation Twyla Harp Consultants

Matter no Account name Matter description

Reason: On account of costs and disbursements

Received by: H. Potter

On behalf of: Potter and Associates

Law Practice
Trust Account

Potter and Associates

Receipt: **71823**

Date: 14/01/20xx

TRUST ACCOUNT RECEIPT

Received from Mr Nat Damon

On 14/01/xx

the sum of Eight hundred and twenty five dollars

$825.00 ~~Cheque~~/Cash~~/Direct Deposit~~

For and on behalf of:

D1	: Damon	: Plea in mitigation
Matter no	Account name	Matter description

Reason: On account of costs and disbursements

Received by: H. Potter

On behalf of: Potter and Associates

Law Practice

Trust Account

Potter and Associates

Receipt: **71824**

Date: 15/01/20xx

TRUST ACCOUNT RECEIPT

Received from Mr James and Mrs Jane Barnes

On 15/01/xx

the sum of One hundred and seventy five thousand dollars

$175,000.00 Cheque/~~Cash/Direct Deposit~~

For and on behalf of: B1 Barnes Purchase Potts Point- $174,000.00

B2 : Barnes : Barnes Sale Point Piper- $1,000.00

Matter no Account name Matter description

Reason: Barnes purchase Potts Point – on account of balance deposit, costs and disbursements

Barnes sale – on account of costs and disbursements

Received by: H. Potter

On behalf of: Potter and Associates

Law Practice

Trust Account

Potter and Associates

Receipt: **71825**

Date: 15/01/20xx

TRUST ACCOUNT RECEIPT

Received from Ms Trina Arena

On 15/01/xx

the sum of Eight thousand dollars

$8,000.00 Cheque/~~Cash/Direct Deposit~~

For and on behalf of:

A1 : Arena : Family court matter – Marco Mendes

Matter no Account name Matter description

Reason: On account of costs and disbursements

Received by: H. Potter

On behalf of: Potter and Associates

Law Practice

Trust Account

Potter and Associates

Receipt: **71826**

Date: 15/01/20xx

TRUST ACCOUNT RECEIPT

Received from Ms Nannette Benning

On 15/01/xx

the sum of Five thousand four hundred and sixty dollars

$5,460.00 ~~Cheque~~/Cash/~~Direct Deposit~~

For and on behalf of:

A2 : Ash : Estate late Angela Ash

Matter no Account name Matter description

Reason: Cash in hand found in home of deceased

Received by: H. Potter

On behalf of: Potter and Associates

Law Practice

Trust Account

Potter and Associates

Receipt: **71827**

Date: 15/01/20xx

TRUST ACCOUNT RECEIPT

Received from Ms Beryl Streep

the sum of One thousand dollars

$1,000.00 Cheque/~~Cash Direct Deposit~~

For and on behalf of:

S1 : Streep : Medical negligence action

Matter no Account name Matter description

Reason: On account of costs and disbursements

Received by: H. Potter

On behalf of: Potter and Associates

Law Practice

Trust Account

Potter and Associates

Receipt: **71828**

Date: 15/01/20xx

TRUST ACCOUNT RECEIPT

Received from Leonard Caprio by telegraphic transfer from Westpac Bank (Melbourne)

On 15/01/xx

the sum of Thirty one thousand five hundred dollars

$31,500.00 ~~Cheque/Cash~~ Direct Deposit

For and on behalf of:

P1	: Paltrow	: Paltrow sale to Caprio
Matter no	Account name	Matter description

Reason: On account 10% deposit

Received by: H. Potter

On behalf of: Potter and Associates

Law Practice

Trust Account

UTS BANK **Credit listing**

Drawer	**Bank**	**Branch or BSB no**	**Amount**
1 Grollow Pty Ltd	Cth	Haymarket	13,000.00
2 Twyla Harp	St George	Kings Cross	2,500.00
3			
4			
5			
6			
7			
8			
9			
10			

Deposit date 15.01.20xx CSO Tellers – initials

Cheques

Trading date | State Cr Tax

Account name

Potter and Associates Law Practice

Trust Account

BSB number **Account Number**

[123-123] [954-3819]

Cheques in this deposit are not available until cleared

Cash breakup

$100	$ **800|00**
$50	$ **|00**
$20	$ **20|00**
$10	$ **|00**
$5	$ **5|00**
Coin	$ **|00**
Total	$ |
Change	|
Total Cash	$ **825|00**

Total Cheques

$15,500.00

Total Cash

$825.00

Total to Credit Summary

$16,325.00

UTS BANK **Credit listing**

Drawer	Bank	Branch or BSB no	Amount
1 J & J Barnes	St George	Bowral	175,000.00
2 Citibank	Citibank	Paddington	8,000.00
3 B Streep	Cth	Beecroft	1,000.00
4			
5			
6			
7			
8			
9			
10			

Deposit date 15.01.20xx CSO Tellers – initials

Cheques

Trading date State Cr Tax

Account name
Potter and Associates Law Practice
Trust Account

Cash breakup		Total Cheques
$100	$ **5000|00**	$184,000.00
$50	$ **400|00**	Total Cash
$20	$ **|00**	
$10	$ **60|00**	$5,460.00
$5	$ **|00**	**Total** to Credit Summary
Coin	$ **|00**	
Total	$ |	$189,460.00
Change	|	
Total Cash	$ **5,460|00**	

BSB number **Account Number**
[123-123] [954-3819]

Cheques in this deposit are not available until cleared

Place finger here (•
to remove cheque
Date: 19/01/xx
Payee: A.S.I.C.

Detail: Reservation of name
H1 – Twyla Harp Incorporation

Chq $35.00

179641

UTS Bank
179641

Date 19/01/xx

Pay A.S.I.C. or bearer
The
sum of Thirty Five Dollars

$35.00

Not Negotiable

Potter and Associates Law Practice TRUST ACCOUNT
ACCOUNT NUMBER 954-3819 /T **H. Potter**

179641•082•000•:•

Place finger here (•
to remove cheque
Date: 19/01/xx
Date 19/01/xx
Payee: Quality Surveyors

Detail: Survey fees
G1 Grollow Pty Ltd – Subdivision
Moore Park

Chq $3,575.00

179642

UTS Bank
179642

Pay Quality Surveyors or bearer
The
sum of Three Thousand Five Hundred and Seventy Five Dollars

$3,575.00

Not Negotiable

Potter and Associates Law Practice TRUST ACCOUNT
ACCOUNT NUMBER 954-3819 /T **H. Potter**

179642•082•000•:•

Place finger here (•
to remove cheque
Date: 19/01/xx
Payee: Woollahra Council

Detail: s 149(2) Certificate
B2 Barnes sale Point Piper

Chq $40.00

179643

UTS Bank

179643

Date 19/01/xx

Pay Woollahra Municipal Council or bearer
The
sum of Forty Dollars

$40.00

Not Negotiable

Potter and Associates Law Practice TRUST ACCOUNT
ACCOUNT NUMBER 954-3819 /T **H. Potter**

179643•082•000•:•

Place finger here (•
to remove cheque
Date: 19/01/xx
Payee: Sydney Water

Detail: Drainage diagram
B2 Barnes sale Point Piper

Chq $20.00

179644

UTS Bank

179644

Date 19/01/xx

Pay Sydney Water or bearer
The
sum of Twenty Dollars

$20.00

Not Negotiable

Potter and Associates Law PracticeTRUST ACCOUNT
ACCOUNT NUMBER 954-3819 /T **H. Potter**

179644•082•000•:•

Trust Account Cash Receipts Book

For period 14 /01/xx to 15/01/xx **Page: 1**

Date Rct/ Rec'd 20xx	Rec no Form	Received from Reason	Account Name Matter no Matter description	Ledger A/c No.	Multi AMT	Rec AMT	Banking Total	Deposit Date
14/01	7182 - 1 Cheque	Grollow Pty Ltd Costs and disbursements	Grollow Pty Ltd Subdivision at Moore Park	G1		13,000.00		
14/01	2 Cheque	Twyla Harp Costs and disbursements	Twyla Harp Incorporation Twyla Harp Consultants Incorporation	H1		2,500.00		
14/01	3 Cash	Nat Damon Costs	Nat Damon Plea in Mitigation	D1		825.00	16,325.00	14/01
15/01	4 Cheque	J & J Barnes Balance deposit, Costs and disbursements	J & J Barnes Purchase Potts Point	B1	174,000.00			
		Costs and disbursements	J & J Barnes Sale Point Piper	B2	1,000.00	175,000.00		
15/01	5 Bank Cheque	Trina Arena Costs and disbursements	T Arena Family Court Matter	A1		8,000.00		
15/01	6 Cash	Nannette Benning Cash in Hand	A Ash Estate late Angela Ash	A2		5,460.00		
15/01	7 Cheque	Beryl Streep Costs and disbursements	B Streep Medical negligence matter	S1		1,000.00	189,460.00	15/01
15/01	8 T/T	Leonard Caprio Deposit	G Paltrow Sale Palm Beach	P1		31,500.00	31,500.00	15/01
			Sub-total carried forward				**237,285.00**	

Trust Account Cash Receipts Book

For period 19 /01 / 01 to 24 / xx / xx **Page: 2**

Date Rct/ Rec'd 20xx	Rec no Form	Received from Purpose	Account name Matter no Matter description	Ledger A/cNo.	Multi AMT	Rec AMT	Banking Total	Deposit Date
			Sub-total brought forward				**237,285.00**	
19/01	7182 - 9 Cheque	J Brabham Proceeds sale m/v	Ash Estate late Angela Ash	A2		12,500.00		
19/01	71830 Cheque	N Collette Costs and disbursements	Collette Collette discrimination matter	C1		2,000.00	14,500.00	19/01
20/01	1 Cheque	Sumi Jo Costs and disbursements	Jo Jo and Summer Bay Opera Theatre	J1		2,750.00		
20/01	2 Cheque	Russell Rowe Disbursements	Rowe Shoplifting charges	R1		440.00		
20/01	3 Cheque	Tom & Nicole Cridman Deposit, costs and disbs	Cridman Cridman purchase Newtown	C2		43,500.00	46,690.00	20/01
24/01	4 Cheque	Kelvin Spacey Costs and disbursements	Spacey Spacey v Almodovar	S2		10,000.00		
24/01	5 Bank Cheque	Alphonse Schwarz Settlement	De Vito De Vito v Schwarz	D3		5,572.50		
24/01	6 Bank Cheque	Ivan Owen Debt collection	Malkovich Malkovich v Owen	M1		15,750.00		
24/01	7 Cheque	Yimou Zhang Deposit, costs and disbs	Yimou Zhang Yimou Zhang for Spielberg	Z1		23,000.00	54,322.50	24/01
			Sub-total carried forward				**352,797.50**	

Trust Account Cash Receipts Book

For Period 26/01/xx to 31/xx/xx **Page: 3**

Date Rct/Rec'd 20xx	Rec no Form	Received from Purpose	Account name Matter no Matter description	Ledger A/c No.	Multi AMT	Rec AMT	Banking	Deposit Date
			Sub-total brought forward				**352,797.50**	
26/01	8 Cheque	Fidel Vista Stamp Duty, Registration and Costs	Humungous Properties Pty – Lease to Vista Unit 1/7 Cook Way, Botany	H4		1,335.00	1,335.00	26/01
28/01	71832	Russell Rowe Cheque dishonoured	Rowe Shoplifting charges	R1		(440.00)	(440.00)	28/01
31/01	71839	AMP Ltd Proceeds life policy	Ash Estate late Angela Ash	A2		15,000.00	15,000.00	01/02
31/01			**Total receipts**				**368,692.50**	

Trust Account Cash Payments Book

For Period 19/01/xx to 27/01/xx **Page: 1**

Date 20xx	Cheque No	Paid to Purpose	Account Name Matter No Matter Description	Ledger A/c No.	Multi AMT	Cheque Amount
19/01	17964 - 1	ASIC Reservation of Name	Twyla Harp Consultants - Twyla Harp Incorporation	H1		35.00
19/01	2	Quality Surveyors Survey Fees	Grollow Pty Ltd Grollow Subdivision Moore Park	G1		3,575.00
19/01	3	Woollahra Council s149(2) Certificate	Barnes Barnes Sale Point Piper	B2		40.00
19/01	4	Sydney Water Drainage Diagram	Barnes Barnes Sale Point Piper	B2		20.00
25/01	5	Seek & Search Pty Ltd Searches	Barnes Barnes Sale Point Piper	B2	50.00	
			T Arena Arena Family Court Matter	A1	275.00	
			A Ash Estate late Angela Ash	A2	40.00	365.00
25/01	6	Steve Boccho Counsel Fees	Collette Collette Discrimination	C1		550.00
26/01	7	Starr Realty Pty Limited Balance Deposit	Cridman Cridman Purchase Newtown	C2		42,000.00
27/01	8	ASIC Incorporation Fee	Twyla Harp Twyla Harp Consultants Incorp	H1		690.00
			Sub-Total Carried Forward			**47,275.00**

Trust Account Cash Payments Book

For Period 28/01/xx to 31/01/xx **Page: 2**

Date 20xx	Cheque No	Paid to Purpose	Account Name Matter No Matter Description	Ledger A/c No.	Multi AMT	Cheque Amount
			Sub-Total Brought Forward			**47,275.00**
28/01	9	Office of State Revenue Stamp Duty on Lease	Humungous Properties Pty Ltd Humungous Properties lease to Vista	H4		855.00
28/01	17965-0	Department of Lands Registration Lease	Humungous Properties Pty Ltd Humungous Properties Lease to Vista	H4		57.00
28/01	1	Drewe De Vito Settlement Balance	De Vito D2 De Vito v Schwarz	D3		4,775.00
28/01	2	Potter Office Account Costs	De Vito D2 De Vito v Schwarz	D3	797.50	
28/01	2	Potter Office Account Costs	Nat Damon D1 Plea in Mitigation	D1	825.00	1,622.50
31/01		**Total Payments**				**54,584.50**
		Cash Book Summary Opening Balance Add Receipts – January Less Payments – January Closing Cash Book Balance	 0.00 368,692.50 54,584.50 314,108.00			

TRUST ACCOUNT TRANSFER JOURNAL

DATE 20xx	JOURNAL REF	AUTHORISED By	ACCOUNT NAME MATTER REFERENCE MATTER DESCRIPTION, PURPOSE	LEDGER A/C No.	DEBIT AMOUNT	CREDIT AMOUNT
29 Jan	J1		Paltrow P1 Sale to Caprio	P1	30,000.00	
		H. Potter	Paltrow P2 Purchase from Renouf (Transfer as directed by client to cover deposit, costs and disbursements)	P2		30,000.00
30 Jan	J2		Cridman C2 Purchase from Dench	C2	1,000.00	
		H. Potter	Cridman C3 Sale Darling Point (Transfer as directed by client to cover costs and disbursements)	C3		1,000.00

TRUST LEDGER

ACCOUNT NAME: Cash Book Control Account

ADDRESS: ______

MATTER NO: ______ **MATTER DESCRIPTION** ______

OTHER PARTY ______

SOLICITOR HANDLING ______ **RESPONSIBLE PARTNER** ______

Date Rct/Rec'd/pd 20xx	Ref No.	Rec'd From/Paid To Jnl To/From Reason	Debit Amount	Credit Amount	Balance
31.01.xx	CRB3	Total Receipts (January)	368,692.50		368,692.50
31.01.xx	CPB2	Total Payments (January)		54,584.50	314,108.00

TRUST LEDGER

ACCOUNT NAME: (Ms) Trina Arena

ADDRESS: 71 Sutherland Road
Paddington

MATTER NO: A1 **MATTER DESCRIPTION** Family Court – Property

OTHER PARTY Marco Mendes

SOLICITOR HANDLING H. Potter **RESPONSIBLE PARTNER** H. Potter

Date Rct/ Rec'd/pd 20xx	Ref No.	Rec'd From/Paid To Jnl To/From Purpose	Debit Amount	Credit Amount	Balance
15.01.xx	R71825	Trina Arena – on a/c Costs Disbursements		8,000.00	8,000.00
25.01.xx	P179645	Seek & Search Pty Ltd Searches	275.00		7,725.00

TRUST LEDGER

ACCOUNT NAME: Estate late Angela Ash (Mrs) Nannette Benning (Executor)

ADDRESS: 2 Norma Crescent

Maroubra

MATTER NO: A2 **MATTER DESCRIPTION** Estate late Angela Ash

OTHER PARTY

SOLICITOR HANDLING H. Potter **RESPONSIBLE PARTNER** H. Potter

Date Ret/Rec'd/ pd 20xx	Ref No.	Rec'd From/Paid To Jnl To/From Purpose	Debit Amount	Credit Amount	Balance
15.01.xx	R71826	N Benning – Cash in Hand		5,460.00	5,460.00
19.01.xx	R71829	J Brabham – proceeds sale car		12,500.00	17,960.00
25.01.xx	P179645	Seek & Search Pty Ltd Searches	40.00		17,920.00
31.01.xx	R71839	AMP Ltd Proceeds Life Policy		15,000.00	32,920.00

TRUST LEDGER

ACCOUNT NAME: (Mr) James and (Mrs) Jane Barnes

ADDRESS: 5 Linlithgow Road

Point Piper

MATTER NO: B1 **MATTER DESCRIPTION** Purchase Rockwall Gardens, Potts Point

OTHER PARTY Rockwall Gardens Pty Ltd

SOLICITOR HANDLING H. Potter **RESPONSIBLE PARTNER** H. Potter

Date Rct/Rec'd/ pd 20xx	Ref No.	Rec'd From/Paid To Jnl To/From Reason	Debit Amount	Credit Amount	Balance
15.01.xx	R71824	J & J Barnes on a/c balance deposit and costs and disbursements		174,000.00	174,000.00

TRUST LEDGER

ACCOUNT NAME: (Mr) James and (Mrs) Jane Barnes

ADDRESS: 5 Linlithgow Road,

Point Piper

MATTER NO: B2 **MATTER DESCRIPTION** Sale 5 Linlithgow Road Point Point Piper

OTHER PARTY

SOLICITOR HANDLING H. Potter **RESPONSIBLE PARTNER** H. Potter

Date Rct/Rec'd/ pd 20xx	Ref No.	Rec'd From/Paid To Jnl To/From Reason	Debit Amount	Credit Amount	Balance
15.01.xx	R71824	J & J Barnes on a/c costs and disbursements		1,000.00	1,000.00
19.01.xx	P179643	Woollahra Council – S149(2) Certificate	40.00		960.00
19.01.xx	P179644	Sydney Water – Drainage Diagram	20.00		940.00
25.01.xx	P179645	Seek & Search Pty Ltd Searches	50.00		890.00

TRUST LEDGER

ACCOUNT NAME: (Ms) Noni Collette

ADDRESS: 2 Diver Crescent,
Porpoise Heads

MATTER NO: C1 **MATTER DESCRIPTION** Discrimination

OTHER PARTY Fantasy Productions Pty Ltd

SOLICITOR HANDLING H. Potter **RESPONSIBLE PARTNER** H. Potter

Date Rct/ Rec'd/ pd 20xx	Ref No.	Rec'd From/Paid To Jnl To/From Reason	Debit Amount	Credit Amount	Balance
19.01.xx	R71830	Noni Collette on a/c costs and disbursements		2,000.00	2,000.00
25.01.xx	P179646	Steve Boccho Counsel's fee	550.00		1,450.00

TRUST LEDGER

ACCOUNT NAME: (Mr) Tom and (Mrs) Nicole Cridman

ADDRESS: 1 Yarra Avenue,
Darling Point

MATTER NO: C2 **MATTER DESCRIPTION** Purchase 85 Watkin Street, Newtown North

OTHER PARTY Maggie Dench

SOLICITOR HANDLING H. Potter **RESPONSIBLE PARTNER** H. Potter

Date Rct/Rec'd/ pd 20xx	Ref No.	Rec'd From/Paid To Jnl To/From Reason	Debit Amount	Credit Amount	Balance
20.01.xx	R71883	T & N Cridman, on account of deposit, costs and disbursements		43,500.00	43,500.00
26.01.xx	P179647	Starr Realty Pty Ltd Balance deposit	42,000.00		1,500.00
30.01.xx	J2	T & N Cridman C3 Sale Darling Point To cover part costs and disbursements	1,000.00		500.00

TRUST LEDGER

ACCOUNT NAME: (Mr) Tom and (Mrs) Nicole Cridman

ADDRESS: 1 Yarra Avenue
Darling Point

MATTER NO: C3 **MATTER DESCRIPTION** Sale 1 Yarra Avenue Darling Point

OTHER PARTY

SOLICITOR HANDLING H. Potter **RESPONSIBLE PARTNER** H. Potter

Date Rct/Rec'd/ pd 20xx	Ref No.	Rec'd From/Paid To Jnl To/From Reason	Debit Amount	Credit Amount	Balance
30.01.xx	J2	T & N Cridman, on account of deposit, C2 Purchase from Dench To cover part costs and disbursements		1,000.00	1,000.00

TRUST LEDGER

ACCOUNT NAME: (Mr) Nat Damon,

ADDRESS: 3 Australia Street,
Camperdown

MATTER NO: D1 **MATTER DESCRIPTION** Plea in Mitigation

OTHER PARTY Police

SOLICITOR HANDLING H. Potter **RESPONSIBLE PARTNER** H. Potter

Date Rct/Rec'd/ pd 20xx	Ref No.	Rec'd From/Paid To Jnl To/From Reason	Debit Amount	Credit Amount	Balance
15.01.xx	R71823	Nat Damon on a/c of cost		825.00	825.00
28.01.xx	P179652	Potter Office Account Costs	825.00		Nil

TRUST LEDGER

ACCOUNT NAME: Drewe De Vito

ADDRESS: 15 Bower Street,
Bankslown

MATTER NO: D3 **MATTER DESCRIPTION** Personal Injury Claim

OTHER PARTY Alphonse Schwarz

SOLICITOR HANDLING H. Potter **RESPONSIBLE PARTNER** H. Potter

Date Rct/Rec'd/ pd 20xx	Ref No.	Rec'd From/Paid To Jnl To/From Reason	Debit Amount	Credit Amount	Balance
14.01.xx	R71835	Alphonse Schwarz Settlement money		5,572.50	5,572.50
28.01.xx	P179651	Drewe De Vito Settlement money	4,775.00		
28.01.xx	P179652	Potter Office Account Costs	797.50		Nil

TRUST LEDGER

ACCOUNT NAME: Grollow Pty Ltd

ADDRESS: 52 Park Street,

Sydney

MATTER NO: G1 **MATTER DESCRIPTION** Subdivision at Moore Park

OTHER PARTY

SOLICITOR HANDLING H. Potter **RESPONSIBLE PARTNER** H. Potter

Date Rct/Rec'd/ pd 20xx	Ref No.	Rec'd From/Paid To Jnl To/From Reason	Debit Amount	Credit Amount	Balance
14.01.xx	R71821	Grollow Pty Ltd on a/c costs and disbursements		13,000.00	13,000.00
19.01.xx	P179642	Quality Surveyors – Survey Fees	3,575.00		9,425.00

TRUST LEDGER

ACCOUNT NAME: (Ms) Twyla Harp

ADDRESS: 2/21 Macleay Street,
Potls Point

MATTER NO: H1 **MATTER DESCRIPTION** Incorporation – Twyla Harp Consultants

OTHER PARTY

SOLICITOR HANDLING H. Potter **RESPONSIBLE PARTNER** H. Potter

Date Rct/Rec'd/ pd 20xx	Ref No.	Rec'd From/Paid To Jnl To/From Reason	Debit Amount	Credit Amount	Balance
14.01.xx	R71822	Twyla Harp on a/c costs and disbursements		2,500.00	2,500.00
19.01.xx	P179641	ASIC – Reservation Name	35.00		2,465.00
27.01.xx	P179648	ASIC – Incorporation Fee	690.00		1,775.00

TRUST LEDGER

ACCOUNT NAME: Humungous Properties Pty Limited

ADDRESS: 19 Bridge Street

Sydney

MATTER NO: H4 **MATTER DESCRIPTION** Commercial Lease Unit 1/7 Cook Way, Botany

OTHER PARTY Fidel Vista

SOLICITOR HANDLING H. Potter **RESPONSIBLE PARTNER** H. Potter

Date Rct/Rec'd/ pd 20xx	Ref No.	Rec'd From/Paid To Jnl To/From Reason	Debit Amount	Credit Amount	Balance
26.01.xx	R71838	Fidel Vista Stamp duty, registration and costs		1,335.00	1,335.00
28.01.xx	P179649	Office of State Revenue Stamp duty on Lease	855.00		480.00
28.01.xx	P179650	Department of Lands Registration fee (Lease)	57.00		423.00

TRUST LEDGER

ACCOUNT NAME: (Ms) Sumi Jo

ADDRESS: 15 Sublime Street,
Leura

MATTER NO: J1 **MATTER DESCRIPTION** Breach of Contract

OTHER PARTY Summer Bay Opera Theatre

SOLICITOR HANDLING H. Potter **RESPONSIBLE PARTNER** H. Potter

Date Rct/Rec'd/ pd 20xx	Ref No.	Rec'd From/Paid To Jnl To/From Reason	Debit Amount	Credit Amount	Balance
20.01.xx	R71831	Sumi Jo on a/c costs and disbursements		2,750.00	2,750.00

TRUST LEDGER

ACCOUNT NAME: Jonathon Malkovich

ADDRESS: 25 Georges Road,
Hurstville

MATTER NO: M1 **MATTER DESCRIPTION** Debt Collection

OTHER PARTY Ivan Owen

SOLICITOR HANDLING H. Potter **RESPONSIBLE PARTNER** H. Potter

Date Rct/Rec'd/ pd 20xx	Ref No.	Rec'd From/Paid To Jnl To/From Reason	Debit Amount	Credit Amount	Balance
24.01.xx	R71836	Ivan Owen – payment of debt		15,750.00	15,750.00

TRUST LEDGER

ACCOUNT NAME: (Ms) Gwen Paltrow

ADDRESS: 6 Pacific Parade

Palm Beach

MATTER NO: P1 **MATTER DESCRIPTION** Sale of 6 Pacific Parade, Palm Beach

OTHER PARTY Leonard Caprio

SOLICITOR HANDLING H. Potter **RESPONSIBLE PARTNER** H. Potter

Date Rct/Rec'd/ pd 20xx	Ref No.	Rec'd From/Paid To Jnl To/From Reason	Debit Amount	Credit Amount	Balance
15.01.xx	R71828	Leonard Caprio on a/c 10% deposit		31,500.00	31,500.00
29.01.xx	J1	Paltrow P2 Purchase from Renouf To cover deposit, costs and disbursements	30,000.00		1,500.00

TRUST LEDGER

ACCOUNT NAME: (Ms) Gwen Paltrow

ADDRESS: C/-7 Riverview Road,
Clareville

MATTER NO: P2 **MATTER DESCRIPTION** Purchase of 2 Jonah Street
Whale Beach

OTHER PARTY Renouf

SOLICITOR HANDLING H. Potter **RESPONSIBLE PARTNER** H. Potter

Date Rct/Rec'd/ pd 20xx	Ref No.	Rec'd From/Paid To Jnl To/From Reason	Debit Amount	Credit Amount	Balance
29.01.xx	J1	Paltrow P1 Sale to Caprio To cover deposit, costs and disbursements		30,000.00	30,000.00

TRUST LEDGER

ACCOUNT NAME: Russell Rowe

ADDRESS: 1 Juno Parade
Alexandria

MATTER NO: R1 **MATTER DESCRIPTION** Shoplifting Charge

OTHER PARTY Police

SOLICITOR HANDLING H. Potter **RESPONSIBLE PARTNER** H. Potter

Date Rct/Rec'd/ pd 20xx	Ref No.	Rec'd From/Paid To Jnl To/From Reason	Debit Amount	Credit Amount	Balance
20.01.xx	R71832	Russell Rowe on account disbursements		440.00	440.00
28.01.xx	R71832	Russell Rowe Receipt Cancelled – dishonoured cheque	440.00		Nil

TRUST LEDGER

ACCOUNT NAME: (Ms) Beryl Streep

ADDRESS: 5 Mason Avenue

Beecroft

MATTER NO: S1 **MATTER DESCRIPTION** Medical Negligence

OTHER PARTY Dr A. Smith and Dr B. Jones

SOLICITOR HANDLING H. Potter **RESPONSIBLE PARTNER** H. Potter

Date Rct/Rec'd/ pd 20xx	Ref No.	Rec'd From/Paid To Jnl To/From Reason	Debit Amount	Credit Amount	Balance
15.01.xx	R71827	Beryl Streep on a/c costs and disbursements		1,000.00	1,000.00

TRUST LEDGER

ACCOUNT NAME: Kelvin Spacey

ADDRESS: 2 Lois Lane

Parramatta

MATTER NO: S2 **MATTER DESCRIPTION** Personal Injury

OTHER PARTY Alberto Almodovar

SOLICITOR HANDLING H. Potter **RESPONSIBLE PARTNER** H. Potter

Date Rct/Rec'd/ pd 20xx	Ref No.	Rec'd From/Paid To Jnl To/From Reason	Debit Amount	Credit Amount	Balance
24.01.xx	R71834	Kelvin Spacey on account costs and disbursements		10,000.00	10,000.00

TRUST LEDGER

ACCOUNT NAME: Yimou Zhang

ADDRESS: 17 Thomas Street,
Haymarket

MATTER NO: Z1 **MATTER DESCRIPTION** Purchase business 'Flights of Fantasy'

OTHER PARTY Stephanie Spielberg

SOLICITOR HANDLING H. Potter **RESPONSIBLE PARTNER** H. Potter

Date Rct/Rec'd/ pd 20xx	Ref No.	Rec'd From/Paid To Jnl To/From Reason	Debit Amount	Credit Amount	Balance
24.01.xx	R71837	Yimou Zhang on account deposit, costs and disbursements		23,000.00	23,000.00

OFFICE ACCOUNT

Potter and Associates
Law Practice — **97071**

10.01.20xx

Received from Harriet Potter ***by*** bank cheque

the sum of Thirty Thousand Dollars

being Capital contribution

Harriet Potter Capital Account PL1

$30,000.00: — ***per H. Potter***

OFFICE ACCOUNT

STANDARD.6298

Potter and Associates
Law Practice — **97072**

19.01.20xx

Received from Edward Hilary ***by*** cheque

the sum of One Hundred and Sixty Five Dollars

being Costs for Will

Hilary: Re Will CL1

$165.00: — ***per H. Potter***

OFFICE ACCOUNT

STANDARD.6298

UTS BANK **Credit listing**

Drawer	Bank	Branch or BSB no	Amount
1 National Australia Bank	NAB	Sydney	30,000.00
2			
3			
4			
5			
6			
7			
8			
9			
10			

Deposit date 10.01.20xx CSO Tellers – initials

Cheques

Trading date State Cr Tax

Account name

Potter and Associates Law Practice

Office Account

BSB number **Account Number**

[123-123] [954-3810]

Cheques in this deposit are not available until cleared

Cash breakup

$100	$	00
$50	$	00
$20	$	00
$10	$	00
$5	$	00
Coin	$	00
Total	$	
Change		
Total Cash	$	00

Total Cheques

$30,000.00

Total Cash

Total to Credit Summary

$30,000.00

UTS BANK **Credit listing**

Drawer	Bank	Branch or BSB no	Amount
1 E Hilary	Westpac	Glebe	165.00
2			
3			
4			
5			
6			
7			
8			
9			
10			

Deposit date 19.01.20xx CSO Tellers – initials

Cheques

Trading date State Cr Tax

Account name

Potter and Associates Law Practice

Office Account

Cash breakup		
$100	$	00
$50	$	00
$20	$	00
$10	$	00
$5	$	00
Coin	$	00
Total	$	
Change		
Total Cash	$	00

Total Cheques

$165.00

Total Cash

Total to Credit Summary

$165.00

BSB number **Account Number**

[123-123] [954-3810]

Cheques in this deposit are not available until cleared

PETTY CASH VOUCHER

Date 14 January 20xx

Matter No. PL7

Client name

Matter

Purpose Office Refreshments

$13.75 *Signature* H. Potter

Place finger here (•
to remove cheque
Date: 14.01.xx
Payee: Telstra

Detail: Telephone Installation
PL2

Chq $1,045.00

555601

UTS Bank

555601

Date 14.01.xx

Pay Telstra or bearer

The
sum of One Thousand and Forty-Five Dollars

$1,045.00

Not Negotiable

Potter and Associates OFFICE ACCOUNT
ACCOUNT NUMBER 123-456 /O **H. Potter**

555601•042•000•:•

Place finger here (•
to remove cheque
Date: 14.01.xx
Payee: Mini Cost Officeworks
Pty Limited

Detail: 2 iMac Computers $4389-PL3;
1 Laser Printer $434.50-PL3; 2 Desks $2090-
PL4; 1 Filing Cabinet $190.30
1 Bookcase $621.50-PL4; Paper $44-PL5
Chq $7,769.30

555602

UTS Bank

555602

Date 14.01.xx

Pay Mini Cost Officeworks Pty Limited or bearer
The
sum of Seven Thousand and Seven Hundred and Sixty Nine Dollars & 30c

$7,769.30

Potter and Associates OFFICE ACCOUNT
ACCOUNT NUMBER 123-456 /O

H. Potter

Not Negotiable

555602•042•000•:•

Place finger here (•
to remove cheque
Date: 14.01.xx
Payee: Cash

Detail: Petty Cash
PL6

Chq $200.00

555603

UTS Bank

555603

Date 14.01.xx

Pay Cash or bearer
The
sum of Two Hundred Dollars

$200.00

Potter and Associates OFFICE ACCOUNT
ACCOUNT NUMBER 123-456 /O

H. Potter

555603•042•000•:•

OFFICE ACCOUNT CASH RECEIPTS BOOK **Page 1**

For Period 10/01/xx to 31/01/xx

DATE OF RECEIPT 2001	RECEIPT NUMBER	CLIENT NAME AND MATTER DESCRIPTION	RECEIVED FROM	PURPOSE OF RECEIPT	LEDGER ACCOUNT NUMBER	CHQ/ CASH	GST	AMOUNT FOR LEDGER Taxable	Non-Taxable	TOTAL ON RECEIPT	BANKING TOTAL AND DATE ON DEPOSIT SLIP
10.01.xx	9707 1	(H. Potter) Capital Account	(H. Potter)	Capital Contribution	PL1	Bank Cheque			30,000.00	30,000.00	30,000.00 10.01.xx
19.01.xx	2	Hilary: Re Will	E Hilary	For Costs	CLH2	Cheque	15.00	150.00		165.00	165.00 19.01.xx
28.01.xx	3	Drewe De Vito De Vito v Schwarz	Potter Trust A/C	For Costs	CLD3	Cheque	72.50	725.00			
	3	Nat Damon Plea in Mitigation	Potter Trust A/C	For Costs	CLD1	Cheque	75.00	750.00		1,622.50	1,622.50 28.01.xx
31.01.xx		**Total Receipts**			**PL 11**		**162.50**	**1,625.00**	**30,000.00**	**31,787.50**	**31,787.50**

OFFICE ACCOUNT CASH PAYMENTS BOOK Page 1

For Period 14/01/xx to 22/01/xx

DATE OF PAYMENT 20xx	CHEQUE NUMBER	CLIENT NAME AND MATTER DESCRIPTION	PAID TO	PURPOSE OF PAYMENT	LEDGER ACCOUNT NUMBER	GST	AMOUNT FOR LEDGER Taxable	Non-Taxable	TOTAL AMOUNT ON FACE OF CHEQUE
14.01.xx	55560-1	Telephone Account	Telstra	Phone Installation	PL2	95.00	950.00		1,045.00
14.01.xx	2	Office Machines Account	Mini Cost Officeworks	2 Computers 1 Laser Printer 2 Desks 1 Filing Cabinet 1 Bookcase 10 pkts Paper	PL3 PL3 PL4 PL4 PL4 PL5	399.00 39.50 190.00 17.30 56.50 4.00	3990.00 395.00 1900.00 173.00 565.00 40.00		7,769.30
14.01.xx	3	Petty Cash	Cash	Petty Cash	PL6			200.00	200.00
22.01.xx	4	Cridman Purchase at Newtown	Speedy Enquiry Service	Searches	CLC2			125.00	125.00
22.01.xx	5	Cridman Purchase at Newtown	Bug-a-lugs Pest Service	Pest Report	CLC2			200.00	200.00
		Sub-Total Carried Forward							**9,339.30**

OFFICE ACCOUNT CASH PAYMENTS BOOK **Page 2**

For Period 23/ 01/xx to 31/01/xx

DATE OF PAYMENT 20xx	CHEQUE NUMBER	CLIENT NAME AND MATTER DESCRIPTION	PAID TO	PURPOSE OF PAYMENT	LEDGER ACCOUNT NUMBER	GST	AMOUNT FOR LEDGER Taxable	Non-Taxable	TOTAL AMOUNT ON FACE OF CHEQUE
		Sub-Total Brought Forward							**$9,339.30**
24.01.xx	55560-6	Spacey v Almodovar Personal Injury	District Court	Filing Fee	CLS2			377.00	377.00
24.01.xx	7	Office Rent	Domain Realty	Rent	PL9	175.00	1,750.00		1925.00
28.01.xx	8	Harriet Potter Drawings	Harriet Potter	Drawings	PL10			550.00	550.00
31.01.xx	9	Cancelled – incorrect entry							
31.01.xx		Bank Charges	UTS Bank	Account Keeping Fee	PL14			100.00	100.00
31.01.xx		**Total Payments**				**976.30**	**9,763.00**	**1,552.00**	**12,291.30**
		Cash Book Summary Opening Balance 0.00 Add Total Receipts 31,787.50 Less Total Payments 12,291.30 Closing Balance 19,496.20							

OFFICE ACCOUNT

PETTY CASH BOOK FOLIO 1

Receipts		Date 20xx		Particulars	Ledger A/C No.	GST	Amount for Ledger		Payments
							Taxable	Non-Taxable	
200	00	Jan	14	OFFICE – Cash					
			14	OFFICE REFRESHMENTS Coffee & Tea	PL6			13.75	13.75
			19	POSTAGE – Stamps	PL8	4.50	40.50	45.00	45.00
			19	STATIONERY – Forms	PL5	7.60	75.95		83.55
			31	**Total Payments (January)**	PL6	12.10	116.45	13.75	**142.30**
				Balance Carried Down					**57.70**
200	00								200.00
57	70	Feb	xx	**Balance Brought Down**					

COSTS JOURNAL – Folio 1

Date 20xx		Client	Particulars	Ledger A/C No.	Amount	
Jan	19	E Hilary	Re Will	CLH1	150	00
Jan	19	Humungous Properties Pty Limited	Lease to Fidel Vista	CLH4	423	00
Jan	28	D De Vito	Personal Injury	CLD3	725	00
Jan	28	N Damon	Plea in Mitigation	CLD1	750	00
Jan	31	**Total Costs (January)**		PL 11	2,048	00

OFFICE ACC. LEDGER (Private)

ACCOUNT NAME: (Harriet Potter) – Capital Account
ACCOUNT NUMBER: PL1

DATE 20xx	Received from or paid to	Purpose	Ref No.	DR		CR		DR/CR	BAL	
Jan 10	Harriet Potter	Initial Capital Contribution	R97071			30,000	00	CR	30,000	00

OFFICE ACC. LEDGER (Private)

ACCOUNT NAME: Telephone
ACCOUNT NUMBER: PL2

DATE 20xx	Received from or paid to	Purpose	Ref No.	DR		CR		DR/CR	BAL	
Jan 14	to Telstra	For installation of telephones	P555601	950	00			DR	950	00

OFFICE ACC. LEDGER (Private)

ACCOUNT NAME: Office Machines
ACCOUNT NUMBER: PL3

DATE 20xx	Received from or paid to	Purpose	Ref No.	DR		CR		DR/CR	BAL	
Jan 14	to Mini Cost Officeworks P/L	4 iMac Computers	P555602	3,990	00			DR	3,990	00
		1 Laser Printer	P555602	395	00			DR	4,385	00

OFFICE ACC. LEDGER (Private)

ACCOUNT NAME: Office Furniture
ACCOUNT NUMBER: PL4

DATE 20xx	Received from or paid to	Purpose	Ref No.	DR		CR		DR/CR	BAL	
Jan 14	to Mini Cost Officeworks P/L									
		Desks	P555602	1,900	00			DR	1,900	00
		Filing Cabinet	P555602	173	00			DR	2,073	00
		Bookcase	P555602	565	00			DR	2,638	00

OFFICE ACC. LEDGER (Private)

ACCOUNT NAME: Stationery
ACCOUNT NUMBER: PL5

DATE 20xx	Received from or paid to	Purpose	Ref No.	DR		CR		DR/CR	BAL	
Jan 14	to Mini Cost Officeworks P/L	White Paper	P555602	40	00			DR	40	00
Jan 19	to Rumpole Law Stationer	Legal Forms	PC1	75	95			DR	115	95

OFFICE ACC. LEDGER (Private)

ACCOUNT NAME: Petty Cash
ACCOUNT NUMBER: PL6

DATE 20xx		Received from or paid to	Purpose	Ref No.	DR		CR		DR/CR	BAL	
Jan	14	Cheque Cashed	Petty Cash	P555603	200	00			DR	200	00
Jan	31	Total Payments (January)		PC1			142	30	DR	57	70

OFFICE ACC. LEDGER (Private)

ACCOUNT NAME: Office Refreshments
ACCOUNT NUMBER: PL7

DATE 20xx	Received from, or paid to	Purpose	Ref No.	DR		CR		DR/CR	BAL	
Jan 14	Petty Cash	Coffee & Tea	PC1	13	75			DR	13	75

OFFICE ACC. LEDGER (Private)

ACCOUNT NAME: Postage
ACCOUNT NUMBER: PL8

DATE 20xx	Received from or paid to	Purpose	Ref No.	DR		CR		DR/CR	BAL	
Jan 19	Petty Cash	Stamps	PC1	40	50			DR	40	50

OFFICE ACC. LEDGER (Private)

ACCOUNT NAME: Office Rent
ACCOUNT NUMBER: PL9

DATE 20xx	Received from or paid to	Purpose	Ref No.	DR		CR		DR/CR	BAL	
Jan 24	To Domain Realty	Office Rent	P555 607	1,750	00			DR	1,750	00

OFFICE ACC. LEDGER (Private)

ACCOUNT NAME: Harriet Potter Drawings
ACCOUNT NUMBER: PL10

DATE 20xx	Received from or paid to	Purpose	Ref No.	DR		CR		DR/CR	BAL	
Jan 20	H Potter	Drawings	P555608	550	00			DR	550	00

OFFICE ACC. LEDGER (Private)

ACCOUNT NAME: Costs Rendered
ACCOUNT NUMBER: PL11

DATE 20xx	Received from or paid to	Purpose	Ref No.	DR		CR		DR/CR	BAL	
Jan 31	**Total Costs (January)**		CJ1			2,048	00	CR	2,048	00

OFFICE ACC. LEDGER (Private)

ACCOUNT NAME: Cash Book Control Account
ACCOUNT NUMBER: PL12

DATE 20xx	Received from or paid to	Purpose	Ref No.	DR		CR		DR/CR	BAL	
Jan 31	**Total Receipts**		CRB 1	31,787	50			DR	31,787	50
Jan 31	**Total Payments**		CPB 2			12,291	30	DR	19,496	20

OFFICE ACC. LEDGER (Private)

ACCOUNT NAME: GST
ACCOUNT NUMBER: PL13

DATE 20xx		Received from or paid to	Ref No.	DR		CR		DR/CR	BAL	
Jan	31	**Total GST received in January**	CRB 1			162	50	CR	162	50
Jan	31	**Total GST paid in January from CB**	CPB 2	976	30			DR	813	80
Jan	31	**Total GST payment from PC**	PC1	12	10			DR	825	90

OFFICE ACC. LEDGER (Client)

ACCOUNT NAME: Tom & Nicole Cridman Purchase Newtown
ACCOUNT NUMBER: CLC2

DATE 20xx	Received from or paid to	Purpose	Ref No.	DR		CR		DR/CR	BAL	
Jan 22	To Speedy Enquiry Service	Searches	P55564	125	00			DR	125	00
Jan 22	To Bug-a-lugs	Pest Report	P55565	200	00			DR	325	00

OFFICE ACC. LEDGER (Client)

ACCOUNT NAME: Nat Damon: Plea in Mitigation
ACCOUNT NUMBER: CLD1

DATE 20xx	Received from or paid to	Purpose	Ref No.	DR		CR		DR/CR	BAL	
Jan 28	To Costs Rendered		CJ1	750	00			DR	750	00
Jan 28	Potter Trust Account	Costs	R97073			750	00	–		Nil

OFFICE ACC. LEDGER (Client)

ACCOUNT NAME: Drewe De Vito: Personal Injury v A Schwarz
ACCOUNT NUMBER: CLD3

DATE 20xx	Received from or paid to	Purpose	Ref No.	DR		CR		DR/CR	BAL	
Jan 28	To Costs Rendered		CJ1	725	00			DR	725	00
Jan 28	Potter Trust Account	Costs	R97073			725	00	–		Nil

OFFICE ACC. LEDGER (Client)

ACCOUNT NAME: E Hilary: Re Will
ACCOUNT NUMBER: CLH2

DATE 20xx	Received from or paid to	Purpose	Ref No.	DR		CR		DR/CR	BAL	
Jan 19	To Costs Rendered		CJ1	150	00			DR	150	00
Jan 19	From Hilary	Costs	P97072			150	00	–	Nil	

OFFICE ACC. LEDGER (Client)

ACCOUNT NAME: Humungous Properties Pty Limited Lease to Fidel Vista
ACCOUNT NUMBER: CLH4

DATE 20xx	Received from or paid to	Purpose	Ref No.	DR		CR		DR/CR	BAL	
Jan 19	To Costs Rendered		CJ1	423	00			DR	423	00

OFFICE ACC. LEDGER (Client)

ACCOUNT NAME: Kelvin Spacey (Personal Injury v Almodovar)
ACCOUNT NUMBER: CLS2

DATE 20xx	Received from or paid to	Purpose	Ref No.	DR		CR		DR/CR	BAL	
Jan 24	To District Court Registry	Filing Fee	P555606	377	00			DR	377	00

Potter and Associates
7 Quay Street, Haymarket 2007

Mrs N Benning
Executor
2 Norma Crescent
MAROUBRA

Trust Statement of Account as at 1.02.xx

Estate late Angela Ash

Date 20xx	Ref No.	Rec'd From/Paid To Jnl To/From Reason	Debit Amount	Credit Amount	Balance
Jan 15	R71826	N Benning – Cash in Hand		5,460.00	5,460.00
Jan 19	R71829	J Brabham – proceeds sale car		12,500.00	17,960.00
Jan 25	P179645	Seek & Search Pty Ltd – Searches	40.00		17,920.00
Jan 31	R71839	AMP Ltd – Proceeds Life Policy		15,000.00	32,920.00

UTS BANKING CORPORATION

222 George Street
Broadway

BANK STATEMENT

Account Name: Potter and Associates Law Practice Trust Account
Account No: 954-3819
Account Address: 7 Quay Street, Haymarket
Statement for period ended 31.1.xx

Date	Particulars	Debit	Credit	Balance
14.01.xx	Balance			0.00
14.01.xx	Deposit		16,325.00	16,325.00 Cr
15.01.xx	Deposit		189,460.00	205,785.00 Cr
15.01.xx	Direct Deposit		31,500.00	237,285.00 Cr
19.01.xx	Deposit		14,500.00	251,785.00 Cr
20.01.xx	Deposit		46,690.00	298,475.00 Cr
24.01.xx	Deposit		54,322.50	352,797.50 Cr
24.01.xx	179642	3,575.00		349,222.50 Cr
24.01.xx	179641	35.00		349,187.50 Cr
25.01.xx	179644	20.00		349,167.50 Cr
26.01.xx	Deposit		1,335.00	350,502.50 Cr
26.01.xx	179646	550.00		349,952.50 Cr
28.01.xx	Dishonoured Cheque	440.00		349,512.50 Cr
29.01.xx	179648	690.00		348,822.50 Cr
29.01.xx	179649	855.00		347,967.50 Cr
30.01.xx	179647	42,000.00		305,967.50 Cr
30.01.xx	179650	57.00		305,910.50 Cr
31.01.xx	179652	1,622.50		304,288.00 Cr
31.01.xx	Interest		25.00	304,313.00 Cr

Potter and Associates
Law Practice
Trust Account
Bank Reconciliation Statement
for month ended 31.01.xx

Balance as per bank statement – 31.01.xx				304,313.00
Add Outstanding Deposits				
Date		**Amount**		
31.01.xx		15,000		15,000.00
Less Bank Credit incorrectly credited				
Date		**Amount**		
30.01.xx		25.00		25.00
				319,288.00
Less Unpresented Cheques				
Date	**Cheque No.**	**Amount**		
19.01.xx	179643	40.00		5,180.00
25.01.xx	179645	365.00		
28.01.xx	179651	4,775.00		
			Balance as per Cash Book	314,108.00

Potter and Associates
Law Practice
Trust Trial Balance
as at 31.01.xx

Matter Number	Account Name	Matter Description	Amount
A1	Arena	Family Court – Property	7,725.00
A2	Ash	Estate late Angela Ash	32,920.00
B1	Barnes	Purchase Rockwall Gardens, Potts Point	174,000.00
B2	Barnes	Sale Point Piper	890.00
C1	Collette	Discrimination	1,450.00
C2	Cridman	Purchase North Newtown	500.00
C3	Cridman	Sale Darling Point	1,000.00
G1	Grollow Pty Ltd	Subdivision Moore Park	9,425.00
H1	Harp	Incorporation	1,775.00
H3	Humungous Properties Pty Limited	Commercial Lease to Vista	423.00
J1	Jo	Breach of Contract	2,750.00
M1	Malkovich	Debt Collection	15,750.00
P1	Paltrow	Sale Palm Beach	1,500.00
P2	Paltrow	Purchase Whale Beach	30,000.00
S1	Streep	Medical Negligence	1,000.00
S2	Spacey	Personal Injury	10,000.00
Z1	Zhang	Purchase Business 'Flights of Fantasy'	23,000.00
			314,108.00

Prepared by H Potter (signed) Dated: 03.02.xx

Clause 72(2)(b)(i) Comparison	
Total Client Ledger	314,108.00
Statutory Deposit	
Reconciled Cash Book	314,108.00
Variance (should be Nil)	

Prepared by: H Potter (signed) **on** 03.02.xx

UTS BANKING CORPORATION

222 George Street
Broadway

Bank Statement

Account Name: Potter and Associates Law Practice Office Account
Account Number: 954-3810
Account Address: 7 Quay Street, Haymarket
Statement for period ended 31.01.xx

Date	Particulars	Debit	Credit	Balance
	Balance			0.00
10.01.xx	Deposit		30,000.00	30,000.00
14.01.xx	555603	200.00		29,800.00
19.01.xx	Deposit		165.00	29,965.00
19.01.xx	555602	7,769.30		22,195.70
24.01.xx	555605	200.00		21,995.70
28.01.xx	555606	377.00		21,618.70
28.01.xx	555608	550.00		21,068.70
29.01.xx	555607	1,925.00		19,143.70
31.01.xx	Bank Charges	100.00		19,043.70

Potter and Associates
Law Practice
Office Account
Bank Reconciliation Statement
for month ended 31.01.xx

Balance as per bank statement –			19,043.70
Add Outstanding Deposits			
Date		**Amount**	
28.01.xx		1,622.50	1,622.50
			20,766.20
Less Unpresented Cheques			
Date	**Cheque No.**	**Amount**	
14.01.xx	555601	1,045.00	1,170.00
22.01.xx	555604	125.00	
		Balance as per Cash Book	19,496.20

Potter and Associates
Law Practice
Office Trial Balance
as at 31.01.xx

Matter Number	Account Name	Matter Description	DR	CR
PL1	Harriet Potter Capital Account	Capital Account		30,000.00
PL2	Telephone	Telephone Account	950.00	
PL3	Office Machines	Machines	4,385.00	
PL4	Office Furniture	Furniture	2,638.00	
PL5	Stationery	Stationery	115.95	
PL6	Petty Cash	Petty Cash	57.70	
PL7	Office Refreshments	Refreshments	13.75	
PL8	Postage	Postage	40.50	
PL9	Office Rent	Rent	1,750.00	
PL10	Harriet Potter Drawings	Drawings	550.00	
PL11	Costs Rendered	Costs Rendered		2,048.00
PL12	Cash Book Control A/C		19,496.20	
PL13	GST		825.90	
PL14	Bank and Charges		100.00	
CLC2	Cridman	Purchase Newtown	325.00	
CLH3	Humungous Properties	Lease to Vista	423.00	
CLS2	Spacey	Personal Injury	377.00	
			32,048.00	32,048.00

Prepared by H Potter (signed) **Dated**: 03.02.xx

OFFICE ACC. LEDGER (Private)

ACCOUNT NAME: Bank Fees and Charges
ACCOUNT NUMBER PL14

DATE 20xx	Received from or paid to	Purpose	Ref No.	DR		CR	DR/CR	BAL	
Jan 31	UTS Bank	Bank changes	CPB2	100	00		DR	100	00

Controlled Money Receipt	
Potter and Associates Law Practice	
Receipt: 1	
Date: 15.01.xx	
Received from: Tim Hanks	
The sum of Nine Thousand Five Hundred Dollars $ 9,500.00 CASH/~~CHEQUE/ DIRECT DEPOSIT~~	
For and on behalf of: Tim Hanks	
Matter No: H3	Matter Description: Personal Injury litigation
Purpose:	To invest with Westpac Bank at call at an interest rate to be determined by Westpac. To be held until disbursements incurred.
Name of controlled money account to be credited:	Potter and Associate, Controlled Money Account Hanks Litigation
Account Number (incl BSB): DO 11395 2037	

by: H. Potter

Name: Harriet Potter

Potter and Associates

Law Practice

Controlled Money Receipt

Controlled Money Receipt

Potter and Associates Law Practice

Receipt: 2

Date: 22.01.xx

Received from: Solita Davidovich

The sum of One Hundred and Seventy Three Thousand, Two Hundred and Forty Nine Dollars and 57 cents $173,249.57

~~CASH~~/CHEQUE/~~ DIRECT DEPOSIT~~

For and on behalf of: Solita Davidovich

Matter No: D2	Matter Description: Estate late Tamara Davidovich
Purpose:	To invest with National Australia Bank at call at an interest rate to be determined by NAB. To be held until distribution of Estate.
Name of controlled money account to be credited:	Potter and Associates Controlled Money Account Davidovich Estate

Account Number (incl BSB): 349-341-790

by: H. Potter
Name: Harriet Potter
Potter and Associates
Law Practice
Controlled Money Receipt

Controlled money movement record
Potter and Associates
Name:___ Tim Hanks____________ __Matter no:___CM1_____
Address____ 15 Hollywood Drive, Birchgrove.
Financial Institution Westpac Bank______________________
Address: Haymarket Branch, 359 George Street, Sydney.
Original investment amount $9,500.00 Date: 15/01/xx
Account name: Potter and Associates Controlled Money Account Hanks Litigation
Account no: DO 11395 2037
Term/duration: at call
INTEREST: Rate 8.2%____________________
Payable from 15/01/xx____________
Payable on: Monthly______________

Date Rct Rec'd/ Paid	**Form & Ref.**	**Pd to/ Received from/ Purpose**	**Auth- Ority**	**Debit W/d**	**Credit Dep.**	**Balance**
15-01 xx	1 Cash	Tim Hanks Investment on a/c disbursements			9,500.00	9,500.00

Controlled money movement record

Potter and Associates

Name: Solita Davidovich ———— **Matter no:** CM2_________

Address 12 Bright Street, Rozelle.____________________

Matter Description Estate late Tamara Davidovich___________________

Financial Institution National Australia Bank________________________

Address: 357 George Street, Haymarket__________________________

Original investment amount $173,249.57 **Date:** 22/01/xx

Account name: Potter and Associates Controlled Money Account Davidovich Estate

____

Account no: 349 341 790_______________________

Term/duration: at call _______________________

INTEREST: **Rate** 8.5% _______________________

Payable from 22/01/xx _______________________

Payable on Monthly _______________________

Date Rct Rec'd Paid	Form & Ref.	Pd to/ Received from/ Purpose	Auth-Ority	Debit W/d	Credit Dep.	Balance
22.01.0x	2 Chq	S. Davidovich Investment Estate Money			173,249.57	173,249.57

Controlled Money Listing
Potter and Associates Law Practice
As at 31.01.xx

Name	Account Name	ADIName/ Account No.	Matter Description	Amount
Hanks T. CM1	Potter and Associates Controlled Money Account Hanks Litigation	Westpac Do 11395 2037	Litigation	$9,500
Davidovich S. CM2	Potter and Associates Controlled Money Account Davidovich Estate	National Australia Bank 349-341-790	Estate	$173,249.57
			Total	$182,749.57

Prepared on 03.02.xx
By Harriet Potter

Power and Eatates Register
Potter and Associates

Data of Power	Name & Address Of Donor	Matter No	Matter Description	Date of death of Deceased.
31.01.xx	Gwen Paltrow	P3	Power of Attorney Bank A/c Commonwealth A/c No. 123–456	

Index